Leasing and Marketing

Leasing and Marketing

Pieter Klaas Jagersma
Toon Sanders

McKinsey & Company

Cover design: Manten Grafische Communicatie&Advies

(Imprint Tilburg University Press)

ISBN 90-361-9806-2

Preface

The annual congress of Leaseurope, the European organization for leasing companies, held in Amsterdam on 9 and 10 October, 1995, was a special occasion for a number of reasons. The Dutch Society for Leasing Companies, as the local organizers, had made a special contribution to the organization. More than in other years the congress had a central theme. Moreover, the choice of theme was daring and challenging: Leasing and Marketing.

Contacts with members had indicated to Leaseurope that the theme of marketing was attracting a great deal of attention. The leasing industry is undergoing major changes, which are demanding increasing management attention. Evolving markets are creating opportunities and threats: opportunities for those who anticipate new openings in time, and threats for companies that ignore the signals from the marketplace.

Against this background, Leaseurope was pleased to help with the survey conducted by McKinsey & Company into the marketing activities of European leasing companies. This survey was carried out amongst Leaseurope members from seven of its associated countries: England, Germany, France, Spain, Italy, Sweden and the Netherlands. The resulting insights into marketing developments in European leasing were presented during the Leaseurope congress in Amsterdam.

Subsequently, the Dutch Association for Leasing Companies started an initiative to produce this book on the congress theme of Leasing and Marketing. The results of the survey forms one chapter, but it mainly contains further work on this theme by authors Pieter Klaas Jagersma of McKinsey & Company and Toon Sanders of the Lage Landen, written after the congress.

Leaseurope greatly welcomes this initiative. This book will undoubtedly make an outstanding opinion-forming contribution to a current "hot topic" for many leasing companies. But it is actually aimed at a much wider audience. The authors have written a book which is of general interest to all those for whom, in one way or another, the subject of leasing and marketing is important.

As Chairman of Leaseurope, I hope that the book will find many interested readers.

A. Dattalo

Chairman of Leaseurope

Foreword by the Dutch Association of Lease Companies (NVL)

Hardly anything has been published on the subject of leasing and marketing. This reflects the gap which obviously exists between the leasing and marketing worlds. But how wide is this gap in practice?

By organizing a congress on the theme "Leasing and Marketing" the NVL, together with Leaseurope, has made an effort to bridge this gap. Also, since there is no doubt that the lease world is showing an ever increasing interest in this subject, the NVL came upon the idea of publishing a book on the theme.

There was however another reason for this publication. Everyone working in the leasing industry knows how much ignorance exists in the industry regarding the various applications of leasing. This ignorance is present in both entrepreneurs and their consultants, who could use a good source to learn more about the possibilities of leasing. The expression "unknown is unloved" applies in this case, and that is a great pity.

The most important reason for publishing this book is perhaps the fact that modern views on marketing are an important source of inspiration for the changes which the industry is currently undergoing. Our objective is not only to build a bridge between the world of leasing and marketing but, to make everyone enthusiastic about bringing the two together.

The NVL sincerely hopes that this book succeeds in meeting its objectives.

Dutch Association of Lease Companies - NVL,

C.A.C.M. Schellens, Chairman

Contents

Introduction

Leasing and marketing

Over the past few years, attention to marketing issues has increased dramatically in the leasing industry. For many leasing company managers, marketing has become a key area of corporate strategy. Markets are changing rapidly, and the management task of exploiting the changes is becoming increasingly difficult. The era of drifting along relying solely on experience and intuition appears to have passed. Customers are making increasingly varied and higher demands, and companies that fail to respond are ruthlessly punished by the market. There is no room anymore for improvisation; a professional approach to marketing issues is imperative.

Demand side

Against this background, it was decided to make the theme of Leasing and Marketing central to the 1995 Leaseurope congress in Amsterdam. Over the two days of the congress, the theme was comprehensively discussed from both the demand and supply side of the leasing industry. The demand side was dealt with by various prominent users of the lease product. Speakers from the market sectors of trucks and trailers, aircraft, property and computers illustrated what leasing meant to their organizations and what they expected of the lease product in the future.

Supply side

The supply side saw the presentation of a set of survey results. Some months before the congress, the first survey into the marketing activities of European leasing companies in seven European countries was conducted by McKinsey & Company.

The findings give interesting preliminary insights into the current thinking and actions of European leasing companies in the field of marketing.

Given the exploratory character of the research and the importance of the subject for the leasing industry, the idea arose to publish this book on the theme of Leasing and Marketing. The survey carried out by McKinsey & Company amongst the European leasing companies is one of the chapters of this book. The results are described in Chapter 4.

Scope and market

Chapter 1 provides a general introduction to the theme of leasing and marketing; Chapter 2 outlines the leasing product and Chapter 3 the market for leasing. The coverage of the McKinsey survey in Chapter 4 is followed by an elaboration on the theme of partnerships with customers in Chapter 5. Finally, Chapter 6 covers the future of the leasing industry.

This book is primarily devoted to business-to-business marketing. Consumer marketing for the leasing product is not yet important enough for it to form a particular focus. Moreover, the book is mainly concerned with the lease market for movable assets, where in practice leasing is used most. Very little attention is paid here to the leasing of property. While property leasing is playing an increasingly important role in the market, coverage of its marketing aspects would demand specific research, which has not been carried out. Likewise, little attention is paid to the market for big ticket leasing. This segment of the market is unusually specialized and the number of suppliers is relatively small.

The organization and operation of this segment of the leasing industry differs from the ordinary lease markets, primarily because special tax concessions are often of overriding importance here.

The aim of this book is to make a wider group aware of the theme of Leasing and Marketing. In other words, the book is not just meant for leasing companies. It is also written for all those who in one way or another are interested in leasing and / or its marketing aspects.

This may include current or future users, as well as government representatives who want to increase their knowledge of the product, in view of the major role played by legislation in the leasing industry. The book is also of interest to consultants whose recommendations are connected with leasing. Furthermore, the book is suitable for business or marketing students who want to know more about the marketing aspects of leasing.

As the book is aimed partly at non-specialists, some parts may not be of great interest to leasing companies. The explanation of the lease product in Chapter 2, for instance, is intended to make clear to the non-specialist what leasing is. For a similar reason, some fairly elementary remarks on marketing are also included. All these parts will contribute to a better understanding of the lease product for non-specialists. If the book succeeds in explaining to the market what can be accomplished in leasing, then the mission of "Leasing and Marketing" has been fulfilled.

Pieter Klaas Jagersma, Heusden

Toon Sanders, Oisterwijk

- *Summer 1996*

Chapter 1 Leasing and Marketing

1.1 INTRODUCTION

In many companies, marketing is regarded as the decisive success factor. The company coming on the market with the right product at the right time will take the biggest slice of the profit. The supplier launching a completely new idea may reap princely rewards. The market holds out the promise of high premiums to organizations whose product range displays evidence of originality and ingenuity.

Thus, marketing is an essential part of business strategy for almost every firm, including leasing companies. However, this fact went largely unacknowledged in the European leasing industry for quite some time. For many years, market conditions were so good that investment in marketing issues was considered by many leasing organizations to be more or less an expensive waste of money. Attention was focused more on operational issues such as effective sales organization and getting the price right. Thinking about future market developments and exploring for new areas of application were not high on the management agenda. In some leasing companies, marketing had no place on the agenda at all.

To understand this attitude properly, we should take a closer look at market conditions in the European leasing industry. The growth of the leasing market only really got properly underway in Europe twenty years ago. European suppliers imported the product from America, so that the introduction of the product to Europe was actually a form of imitation rather than product innovation.

This meant that European suppliers were able to add to the successful applications that had been realized with this product in America. Moreover, the product in Europe twenty years ago was at the beginning of its life cycle and thus still offered the market plenty of opportunities for growth. It is understandable under the circumstances that marketing issues did not head the priority list.

At first, leasing was mainly used in Europe as a supplementary financial instrument. Applications were developed to fill gaps in the existing financial offering, often serving companies which did not have the financial vigor to cover all their needs through the banks. In such situations, leasing can be used to generate extra financial scope on the basis of the asset value of investment objects. This application acts as an extension of the finance company, and does not directly invoke the need for extra marketing effort.

A further reason why marketing was low on the agenda was the tax situation. Various countries have, in the past, applied fiscal measures to boost the economy which encouraged not only investment, but also the use of leasing. Once more, marketing was not an issue. Indeed, however much the leasing industry may have profited from such measures, they undoubtedly put curbs on any development of marketing creativity.

It would be little exaggeration to say that in certain countries the tax authorities were sometimes the most important sales promoter. This obviously created a certain dependency on favorable taxation measures, and did nothing to stimulate the leasing companies' own ability to shape the added value of the lease product.

The supply structure of the industry also relegated marketing to a subordinate role. As the leasing industry developed in Europe, many small leasing organizations with a strong focus on the local and/or regional market place grew up. In general, such companies do little marketing. They usually have a good insight into the regional market, and relations with the customer are often based on long-standing contacts. And unless these local and regional markets change radically, there is little incentive to put much energy into marketing activities.

1.2 POSITIONING MARKETING IN THE LEASING INDUSTRY

However, times have changed. Markets are evolving in many ways, and it is becoming increasingly important for leasing companies to start thinking about marketing.

One important change, for example, is that the times of structurally high economic growth in Europe seem to have passed. In Western Europe in particular, increasingly clear indications of saturation are appearing in the leasing market. This saturation is being caused not only by slackening economic growth, but also by growing competition. These two factors combined are putting profits under increasing pressure. The resulting fall in profitability is forcing leasing organizations to think about different, more creative marketing solutions.

It is also clear that markets are becoming more and more dynamic. Modern technology means a constant flow of new products. The process of economic obsolescence of many capital goods is thus being stepped up. Moreover, modern information and communication technology allow knowledge and information about new products to spread around the world with increasing speed. The domain of international competition is thus expanding at a rapid pace. Gone are the days when local suppliers were assured of a reasonably safe existence in the local market. More and more products are finding their markets internationalizing; consequently, insights are needed into the development of international markets. More attention needs to be paid to marketing for all these reasons.

Marketing has a specific definition in the leasing industry, due to the nature of the lease product. A lease is an intermediate form between buying and hiring, and has characteristics of both. We will expand on this point further in the following chapter. A hybrid product calls for hybrid marketing, sharing elements with two different markets: buying and hiring. Leasing could thus be described in marketing terms as a mixed market.

Indeed, we may legitimately wonder whether leasing is a separate market at all, or whether it is merely a derivative of the buying or the hire market.

A second important fact in this context is that leasing is a form of service, and does not stand alone. Leasing is always linked to the sale of a specific physical product or products. It always entails object-related financing. This means that in the marketing of leasing we are faced with a second mixed form: it has features of both service marketing and industrial marketing.

Therefore, it is no simple matter to apply the concept of marketing to leasing. For a clear understanding of its position in this industry, we have to consider in detail the relationship between the provision of services and the provision of goods that is involved here.

The analysis of service provision by Kotler and Andreasen provides a good insight into the relationship between the two.[1] They have

---

1 Kotler, P. and A. Andreasen: "Strategic Marketing for Non-Profit Organizations", Prentice Hall, Englewood Cliffs, NY. 1991

identified three different product levels for service provision: the core product, the tangible product and the augmented product.

If we take the purchasing of a car as an example, the car is the core product (defined as the product which meets a specific need).[2] The way in which that product is executed is called the tangible product. This is the second product level and includes all tangible and openly visible characteristics of the product such as styling, packaging, brand name and quality.

The third product level is the augmented product. This is the tangible product plus additional services and benefits, included to satisfy additional consumer needs, and/or to differentiate a product further from its competitors. Many of these additional features tend to be services such as pre-sales and after-sales service, guarantees, etc.

It is clear where leasing belongs in this hierarchy of products: it is a typical part of the augmented product. Marketing in the leasing industry can thus be approached from two angles. It can be viewed as a derivative function for the benefit of the sales of the core product. From this point of view, the main issue is: how can the lease product make the optimum contribution to the stimulation of sales of the core product? This line of approach largely fits in with the use of leasing as an instrument for sales financing.

The second angle of approach is: how can the lease product best be sold in the market as the provision of a service. Where do the market opportunities for leasing lie, what new forms of service offer market opportunities, and how can these products best be sold in the market?

This angle is wider, and in fact includes all possible forms of application of leasing, including those which have not yet been developed.

1.3 WHAT IS MARKETING?

Marketing can be defined in many different ways. Broadly speaking, marketing can be said to include all those activities which contribute to an optimum match between the offering of a certain market participant on the one hand and the needs of the customer on the other. The supplier aims to earn a certain economic benefit by offering his products or services.

When making his choice, the customer will often aim for an optimum price/quality ratio. It is therefore difficult in practice to determine

2 Derived from Palmer, A. "Principles of Services Marketing", Mc Graw-Hill Books International 1994, p.25

precisely the level at which the two parties will reach the optimum position. It is, however, clear that the supplier will be aiming to keep his customer happy in the long term, while himself earning as large an economic benefit as possible.

The content and priority of the marketing function depend partly on the market conditions at a specific point in time. Just how much this applies to the development of the European leasing market has been discussed above.

In times when the market shows reasonable growth opportunities, marketing priorities will lie elsewhere than under stagnation. In connection with this, the following three types of market orientation can be distinguished: product orientation, sales orientation, and marketing orientation. [3]

In markets with plenty of sales potential, firms will concentrate on adjusting production capacity to the opportunities offered by the market. Suppliers are thus production oriented, and attention to marketing issues will be limited.

Where demand is more restricted, the supplier will intensify his sales efforts, bringing into play advertisements, promotions and action (extra) commercial capacity. Such companies are sales oriented.

A third type of enterprise is the marketing oriented enterprise. This type of firm concentrates on getting the right product to the right market at the right time. This marketing philosophy was developed in the fifties by American organizations and now also applies internationally as the most accepted definition of marketing.

In the marketing oriented environment, suppliers aim to meet the wishes and desires of closely defined target groups on a sustainable basis. In our examination of the leasing market, we assume that this is the most appropriate orientation for the leasing industry to the marketing phenomenon. This approach includes more than just the familiar customer-oriented marketing.

Three branches of a marketing oriented approach can be identified:

- *Customer orientation*: an organization needs to have sufficient understanding of its target customers to allow it to create superior value to them. Such value consists of increasing the benefits to the buyer in relation to the buyer's costs, or by cutting the buyer's costs

---

3 Derived from Palmer, A. "Principles of Services Marketing", Mc Graw-Hill Books International 1994, page 27.

in relation to the buyer's benefits. A customer orientation requires the organization to understand value to the customer not only as it is today, but also as it will evolve over time;

- *Competitor orientation*: this is defined as the organization's understanding of the short-term strengths and weaknesses and the long-term capabilities and strategies of current and potential competitors;
- *Inter-functional coordination*: this refers to the manner in which an organization uses its resources in creating added value for target customers. An organization contains many individuals with responsibility for creating value, and a marketing orientation requires the organization to draw on and integrate its human and physical resources effectively and adapt them to meet customer needs.

It is extremely important for the marketing approach to consider these three aspects in conjunction. Naturally, the focus is on the customer, but it is not on the customer alone. Just as much attention, if not more, has to go to competitors and to your own organization. A permanent relationship with the client can only be established if you succeed in fulfilling the customer's desires better than competitors do.

Permanently monitoring the needs of the client is one of the basic precepts of modern management. Following up on changes is another: translating the client's needs into market opportunities is a challenge for the whole organization. With a modern marketing orientation there is no room for a half-hearted approach to marketing issues; marketing is integrated into the whole of the organization.

1.4 MARKETING OF SERVICES

We pointed out above that the concept of marketing in the leasing industry shares common ground with both industrial (product) and services marketing. When most people think of marketing, they think of the marketing of goods. The marketing of services is a very recent development. For our present purposes, it is therefore appropriate to pay particular attention to the subject of services marketing.

Services marketing differs in a number of ways from the common forms of product marketing, such as industrial marketing and consumer marketing, a phenomenon partly to be explained by the differences in value delivery between goods and services.

First, delivering a service usually does not involve physical provision. Services often consist of 'a bundle of benefits to the customer'. They are often based on an 'experience' and not a 'thing'. Services are intangible.

Second, with services production and consumption often take place simultaneously. With goods the two usually take place separately. Goods can be produced for stock; with services this is usually impossible. Moreover, with service provision the customers are often involved themselves to a certain extent with production as well as consumption. This phenomenon may be described as interactive consumption, i.e., the customer and the provider jointly determine the quality of the product provided.

Take a visit to a restaurant, for example. The atmosphere the owner wishes to create depends partly on the behavior of the visitor. This is very different from the marketing of goods, where the producer basically has the quality of the product permanently under his own control.

Similarly, in services the effort of the employees also determines the quality of the end product to a large extent. This is not just a question of objective quality standards in terms of education, knowledge and experience. It also entails the frame of mind which the service provider, through his behavior, induces in his customer. Can he create a certain feeling of trust? Does he know how to capture the customer's loyalty, to form an enduring relationship with him?

It is the customer's subjective quality perception that concerns us here. If the provision of a service meets high objective quality standards, but the client does not experience it as such, then the service provision still falls short. Services are to a large extent "people businesses", and the relationship between supplier and customer is largely determined by what the customer grants the supplier.

The degree of personal involvement varies widely among the different forms of service provision, a factor which makes the product very heterogeneous. Services where personal involvement is very high generally do not lend themselves at all well to standardization.

Leasing covers a wide spectrum in this regard. Concluding some leases is more or less routine, and the personal contribution of the seller or advisor is negligible. Accordingly, this sort of transaction lends itself very well to standardization. With more complex leases the personal contribution of the advisor will carry great weight and will often even be the deciding factor.

Time is another major factor in the quality of service provision. In financial services this factor is always very important, sometimes just as much as the personal contribution. Speed of closure is of overriding importance to some customers.

This applies to leasing, for example, in cases where it is offered at the "point-of-sale", e.g., at car and truck dealers. Speed and ease are often the decisive factors why a customer chooses a lease solution here, without bothering to look into other alternatives.

In conclusion, it can be noted that with services a number of new dimensions not involved in the marketing of goods are added to the marketing concept, giving the marketing of services a complete identity of its own.

Since, as we have said, leasing is a form of service, these dimensions are also involved in the marketing of leasing. However, the extremely heterogeneous nature of the lease product makes it difficult to define the role they play.

One factor that does emerge clearly, however, is that the concept of quality has more aspects with services than with goods. These can be summarized under the following three headings: what is being supplied (the technical quality), how it is being supplied (the functional quality) and by whom is it being supplied (the relational quality). [4]

It is of crucial importance to know the aspects on which the customer's quality perception is based. The significance of the aspects listed above to each customer will differ according to the nature of the service. Only detailed and reliable information about the wishes and desires of the customer can indicate which factors carry the most weight for which services, including the different forms of leasing.

1.5 THE MARKETING MIX IN THE LEASING INDUSTRY

The set of tools available to a supplier to realize his marketing objectives is called the marketing mix. These tools can be used for both short and long term objectives.

The concept of the marketing mix is best known in the form of the so-called "four Ps": product, price, place and promotion. The ideas around these four Ps date back to the fifties and were primarily de-

[4] De Vries, Kasper, Van Heldingen: "Dienstenmarketing", Stenfert Kroese, 1994, page 16

veloped for the benefit of industrial marketing. However, they are not sufficient on their own in the context of services marketing.

Moreover, services marketing often demands a different way of applying the tools. In the following sections, we outline the elements needed to supplement the marketing mix in the case of services.

Leasing companies have to take a wide range of factors into account in the execution of the marketing mix. We have already mentioned the complex character of the marketing concept in the leasing industry, due to its mixture of elements from related markets.

The issue is further complicated by the mode of distribution. Leasing often uses indirect forms of distribution. In vendor leasing, for example (see Chapter 2), a leasing company delivers its service indirectly to the end user, via the supplier of the physical product. In such cases, a leasing company has to deal with two sorts of customer relationships, as it were: the producer / supplier and the end user (the customer for the core product). Each of these demand different execution of the marketing mix.

Defining the marketing mix for leasing companies, then, is no simple matter. Every leasing company will have to devise a suitable mode of execution to fit its own situation. The way in which this execution is designed is by way of being the "chef's secret". Finding the ideal mix means being the most successful player. The following sections summarize the most important elements of the marketing mix, in as far as they apply to leasing companies.

1.5.1 PRODUCT

The "product" can be described here as the service which a leasing company offers its customer. As indicated above, this product can be approached from different angles. Following on from the above analysis, we will use three quality dimensions: technical, functional and relational quality.

Technical quality describes what is being supplied. In the leasing industry, this consists of three elements: financing, supplementary object services, and supplementary information services. These subjects are covered in more detail in the next chapter.

So far, information services are rarely used in service provision, but with the arrival of the digital information highway and the development of the "virtual market", this area will undoubtedly grow rapidly in the future.

Functional quality is concerned with how the product is supplied. This includes such aspects as: channel of distribution, the level of personal contribution when delivering the service, and the speed with which the service is delivered. The elements of personal involvement and speed are typical parts of the marketing mix which are missing from the traditional four Ps. They are, however, just as essential to the marketing of services as the original four.

Relational quality is concerned with who the supplier is. This includes all aspects of the manner in which personal service delivery is offered to the customer.

1.5.2 PRICE

Two different categories can be defined in price setting: financial services and non-financial services. The rates in financial services are largely dictated by the market.

Increasing competition in the leasing industry is putting more and more pressure on margins, and is also making price comparisons more and more simple. Pricing policy is based on a cost-plus model, where extra premiums are calculated depending on the size of the contract and the degree of risk. With non-financial services, the most important difference is in the application of open or closed calculation (see also Chapter 2).

1.5.3 PROMOTION

There is a big difference between the promotion of industrial goods and the promotion of services. Services are intangible; a manufacturing company always has a visible product. The question of how a service company gives substance to this aspect of the marketing mix depends very much on the type of service delivery. Sometimes the emphasis is on the image of the organization. This can be very useful for companies with a clear quality difference in this area. On the international European market, however, this strategy is not suitable for every company. It is very costly to establish an international name from a relatively backward position.

This aspect can naturally be exploited in cases where the personal quality of the service delivery is very important. The development of networks of relationships with customers and potential customers is very important in the leasing industry. Thus, sponsorships and relationship marketing will form an increasingly large share of promotion policy.

1.5.4 PLACE

Another element of the marketing mix is location. This aspect is only of interest to the marketing function if a relationship exists between the service provider and the client. This is by no means always the case with leasing. A leasing company's headquarters often only accommodates back-office activities and the management apparatus.

For leasing companies using third party distribution channels (suppliers, banks, dealers), the location is of little marketing consequence. The further development of modern information and communication technologies will undermine its importance even further. In contrast, the way in which distribution is organized will come more and more to the fore.

1.5.5 PEOPLE

The most crucial difference between a manufacturing company and a service company lies in the importance of the human factor. For a buyer of, for example, a car, the people who produced it are completely irrelevant. In service companies, the personal contribution is often decisive.

The extent to which personal factors play a role can vary dramatically in services. Personal factors carry much less weight when picking up a McDonald's sandwich than when eating a meal at an exclusive restaurant. The heterogeneity in service provision is enormous.

This also applies to leasing companies. The services delivered range from completely standard and impersonal contracts to deals totally customized to the wishes of an individual customer. The trend in the market is that the customer is demanding more and more customization. More customization does not, however, necessarily entail more personal contribution.

Customized goods can also be organized from the back office in a more standardized way. In the future, with the growth of modern information and communication technology, this phenomenon will undoubtedly increase even more dramatically. Undoubtedly, the back office will have to talk more to the customer in future. Making such communications flow smoothly is, of course, very important from a marketing point of view.

The people aspects cover a wide range of quality measures. These include not only staff knowledge and experience, but also the entire package of a positive attitude to service and the way a company communicates with its customers. To be able to perform these functions adequately, a company must first identify the market segments it is operating in, and find out what the customer expects in terms of personal service provision. In fact, this demands a continuous audit of the people quality dimensions of service delivery and a plan of action to make necessary improvements. Part of this is a good development and training program.

1.5.6 PARTNERSHIP

The nature of the leasing company means it must work together with a large number of parties in the market. This is partly due to the character of the augmented product: leasing is a tool to support the sales of a core product. To perform this function well, the supplier of the lease product will have to build an outstanding relationship of cooperation with the producer/supplier. This has to mean a partnership at all levels, i.e., shaping the relationship in such a way that both parties experience lasting benefit from working together.

A partnership depends on an attitude which focuses on give and take and respect for each other's interests. In any case, chasing after short term successes has no part to play here. 'Partnership management' is a business philosophy, which must emanate from top management and be supported by the whole organization. Partnerships within the organization are just as important as the external partnerships.

Without internal partnerships, external partnerships are hard to imagine. In practice, working together often also leads to contacts at various levels in the organization. A real partnership only exists if the parties concerned feel that they are a perfect fit.

1.6 STRATEGIC MARKETING ISSUES

Strategic issues are related to the company's positioning in the market, i.e., the choice of what type of goods or services a company wants to operate with on which market or markets.

It has long been common practice to approach strategic marketing issues from a product-oriented point of view. Strategies were focused on industries and products. With this approach, a strategy was typified by the choice of the branch of industry in which a company wanted to conduct its activities, as well as the type of goods or services it wished to offer.

Igor Ansoff's product/market matrix is well known in this context, and is still often applied.[5] The matrix indicates different routes for the development of a business strategy. Taking as its premise a company's existing product/market position, it illustrates several options: a company can opt to seek new markets for existing products (market development). These new markets could involve geographically new markets (for instance via export, or by opening a foreign branch), but also new areas of application for existing products. An example of the latter in the leasing industry is leasing for investments in intangible assets.

Another direction in the strategy matrix is product development: adding new elements to existing products, thus increasing the added value. An example of this in the leasing industry is the service lease: extending the existing lease product by services such as repairs, maintenance and insurance.

A third direction is diversification: entering new markets with new products. 'New' in this case means new for the company, not new for the market. Diversification strategies have often been used in situations where there was too little room to expand in the existing markets. It was also regarded as a way of spreading risks: "don't put all your eggs in one basket".

Some companies that have been highly successful in applying this strategy. In the USA, General Electric has succeeded in expanding from an electricity utility into a major and successful conglomerate. This shining example has inspired many imitators, but by no means all of them have been successful.

British Aerospace attempted to deploy its strong financial position in the defense industry to build up positions in the automotive industry (Rover), construction (Ballast Nedam), and real estate. The results were extremely disappointing and, as a consequence, these interests have now been sold. Expectations with regard to synergy effects (2+2=5) proved largely theoretical. Instead of synergies bringing rewards, profits in many cases slumped rapidly. Daimler-Benz, too,

5 M. Igor Ansoff: "Corporate Strategy", Mc Graw-Hill Books International, 1965

found this out to its cost when it attempted to build a global position in high-tech sectors such as the automotive industry, the aircraft industry, microelectronics, communications and energy. The attempt to expand the company into a diversified global conglomerate led to the deepest crisis in the history of its existence.

Failed diversification strategies have brought about a turnaround in the thinking on strategic issues. An over-emphasis on concepts such as large, strong and powerful, gave way to consideration of the core activities of an enterprise.

Before defining strategic market positions, a company first needs to be clear about the features from which it draws its competitive advantage. Michael Porter has done pioneering work in this area. [6]He made it clear that companies should not necessarily be regarded as suppliers of a certain number of products. Companies create value on the market, and this value is made up of a number of components. The creation of value by a business can be described in terms of a value chain. This consists of a collection of logically ordered activities, which may be divided into five categories: inbound logistics, operations, outbound logistics, marketing and sales, and service.

The significance of each category for the value creation of the business can be determined. In addition, the extent to which a business possesses competitive advantages in those categories can be analyzed. In this manner, the strengths and weaknesses of a business in essential quality features are revealed. This, as it were, is the foundation on which a business can further develop its qualities. It also gives direction to the strategic choices that a company should make.

Mapping out the core qualities of a business is an essential prerequisite for good strategic policy. However, it is not sufficient in itself. The key issue is the extent to which a company is able to translate these core qualities into profitability in the market. This will depend on the scope the market has to offer.

A company with strong advantages in a largely saturated market will, in many cases, be insufficiently rewarded for these advantages. After all, a 'me-too' supplier does not earn such healthy margins as a successful innovator. Corporate strategy, therefore, is partly about occupying promising strategic positions in good time.

Competitive differentiation, therefore, is not sufficient on its own; the profit premium which can be obtained with unique competitive

---

6 Michael E. Porter: "Competitive Advantage", The Free Press, 1985

advantages is often much more important. Strategically unique positions are not, as a rule, due to coincidence. They are the result of the following corporate qualities:

- *market vision*: insight into the structure and composition of the market, and the capacity to see where it is heading in the future;
- *strategic decisiveness*: the ability to translate the market vision into strategic choices at the right time;
- *innovativeness*: the development and timely market launch of new products and services. This is really a matter of translating the core capabilities of a business on the one hand into concrete, attractive commercial opportunities on the other.

The future is therefore an important dimension of strategic policy. The company with the best ability to predict the future also has the best qualifications to win the competitive battle. Future-oriented thinking thus forms the basis of strategic policy. The issue is then: how predictable is that future?

Important work has been done in this area by Gary Hamel and C.K. Prahalad. [7] Their publication "Competing for the Future" examined the strategic policies of a large number of companies. Their research particularly focused on the extent to which companies were able to adapt their offerings to changing circumstances in time.

The essence proved to lie in the concept of core competence: the aggregation of corporate knowledge, expertise and experience which allowed it to meet ever-changing market demands at the right time. Core competencies are not defined in terms of the product offering. The product offered by a company at a given point in time is the core business.

A light-bulb manufacturer produces light-bulbs, and that is its core business. Its core competence is meeting the customer's demand for lighting. A company which has good insights into the customer's demands and can also see where these demands are trending will be able to develop its core competence in the right direction at the right time. It offers, so to speak, "lighting solutions".

According to recent thinking in the area of strategic policy, companies are much more providers of solutions for certain customer needs than

---

7 Gary Hamel and C.K. Prahalad: "Competing for the Future", Harvard Business School Press, 1994

suppliers of a set of products. Companies have core competencies in order to offer good solutions to these needs at the right time.

Customer needs are not static givens, but are changing all the time. The company's task to develop its core-competencies in the right direction in the interests of the customer is therefore never finished. To the contrary, product innovation is getting faster every day, and ever more effort and energy is needed to keep up the pace. It is essential here for the company to be assured that its strategic management has all the information it needs to choose the right strategic positions at the right time.

In strategic terms, then, as well as others, companies are constantly thinking about the customer, and asking themselves with every day that passes how they can improve their performance for the benefit of the customer. As a company develops more and better qualities, it will also become more successful in developing its core-competencies well.

The future-oriented dimension of strategic policy thus takes on a more tangible character. Sailing on the compass of things to come no longer means groping in the dark, but is more a matter of heading for a visible beacon. Predicting the future makes the transition, so to speak, to taking a hand in shaping that future. Successful companies are those which, strategically speaking, are able to create their own future.

Chapter 2 Leasing: the product and the market

2.1 *INTRODUCTION*

This chapter outlines the most important features of leasing. As well as defining the content of the lease product, we will also indicate the factors motivating customers to use it. We will start with an overview of the nature and size of the leasing market.

2.2 *THE SIZE OF THE MARKET*

Leasing is an important financial instrument for investing in capital goods. The volume of the global market in terms of new contracts concluded is more than US$ 300 billion per annum. The US has a share of about 40% of this volume, and Europe and Asia each have a share of 25%. The following table illustrates the significance of leasing world-wide compared to other financial instruments (box 2.1).

Box 2.1 *(Source: Euromoney Capital Markets)*

GLOBAL CAPITAL MARKET VOLUMES (US$ BILLION)			
	1991	**1992**	**1993**
Loans	559	627	795
Leasing	345	323	310
Euro bonds	248	290	409
Euro commercial paper	55	26	28
Medium-term notes	46	104	110
Euro notes	4	6	4
International equities	22	25	40

The leasing market has grown considerably in the last 15 years. Compared to 1984, the volume of leases in the United States has more than doubled. In Europe, the volume of leasing contracts has actually quadrupled since 1984. Some years ago Europe appeared to be a stagnating market, due, amongst other factors, to the recession. In the meantime, however, the downturn has been reversed, signalling a new period of growth.

This growth is not expected to reach the highs of the 1980s, when the European version of the product was still right in the middle of the expansion phase of the product life cycle. It is felt that the European leasing market now appears to be showing some signs of saturation, although there is no objective evidence for this as yet. The level of penetration of leasing is still lower in Europe than in the US, for example.

On the basis of the figures published in the World Leasing Yearbook 1995, the penetration level of leasing in the States is 32%. No European country has more than 20% penetration, with the exception of Ireland where the figure is strongly influenced by the tax conditions peculiar to that country. These figures suggest that leasing has not yet reached its ceiling in Europe.

The strongest growth in leasing will be in the emerging markets such as South America, South-East Asia, and Eastern Europe. In countries such as China, India, Argentina, Chile, and Brazil, enormous investment programs in infrastructure, housing construction and industry are in the pipeline. US and European companies will make a considerable contribution to these investments, and it is certain that leasing as a financing instrument will also play a major role.

2.3 *THE DEMAND SIDE*

The most important outlet for leasing is the professional market, which consists of trade and industry and government. Leasing also plays a small role in the market for private customers, and this role is unlikely to grow in the foreseeable future. Leasing is principally an instrument for investing in capital goods, and therefore the professional market will continue to be its main focus. Box 2.2 shows the structure of the leasing market in Europe.

Box 2.2 *(Source: Leaseurope Annual Report (1993; 1994))*

COMPOSITION OF NEW LEASING CONTRACTS CONCLUDED FOR EQUIPMENT BY BUSINESS SECTORS IN EUROPE, 1992-1994, %

	1992	**1994**
Agriculture	3,0	3,2
Manufacturing/construction	35,8	38,2
Service private sector	47,3	42,4
Service public sector	5,2	4,6
Consumer	5,7	7,6
Other	3,0	4,0

These figures make it clear that the industrial and commercial services sectors are by far the most important market sectors for leasing.

They also indicate growth in the private sector, even though its market share remains small. This development is probably linked to increasing acceptance of the phenomenon of "leasing". It is to be observed that more and more private sector companies are discovering new areas of application for leasing, which are also being actively propagated via promotional activities.

2.4 *TYPE OF GOODS FOR LEASING APPLICATION*

Leasing is applied to many different categories of goods, its main area of application being moveable assets, such as automobiles, trucks, and production machinery. As self-contained, easily identifiable goods served by an efficient second-hand market, they are well suited to leasing. However, the field of application for leasing is not exclusively limited to readily marketable goods. Less marketable goods or even non-marketable goods may also be leased, although the residual value risk then carries more and more weight.

Leasing is a lively and creative market which sometimes comes up with highly original areas of application. An example of this is the so-called 'technolease' which is used in the Netherlands by Rabobank at Philips and Fokker. This involves the sale-and-lease-back of company know-how in the form of charters and patents. Such material constitutes intangible assets, for which there is normally no ready second-hand market and which are therefore difficult to value with any accuracy. This is a highly exceptional form of leasing from the point of view of product development.

In addition to the above, leasing is applied to investments in commercial real estate, for new as well as existing buildings. The scope for this form of leasing is strongly influenced by prevailing legislation, which can vary widely from country to country. The composition of the real estate portfolio of European leasing companies is as follows (box 2.3).

Box 2.3 *(Source: Leaseurope Annual Report (1994))*

TYPE OF REAL ESTATE IN THE PORTFOLIO OF EUROPEAN LEASING COMPANIES, 1994, %

	1994
Company premises	26,3
Shop premises	26,3
Office buildings	28,6
Hotel and recreation premises	2,2
Government buildings	4,4
Other	12,2

2.5 THE SUPPLY SIDE

The supply side of the lease market can be divided up into three categories: (1) bank affiliated leasing companies, (2) captives, and (3) other independent leasing companies and intermediaries.

Bank-affiliated leasing companies are subsidiaries of banks which present themselves on the market as brand-independent general leasing companies. Their leasing activities are often an extension of their parent companies' banking services and consist predominantly of finance leases. The last few years have witnessed an increasing trend towards specialization in the leasing sector, which is also evident in bank-affiliated leasing companies. General leasing companies are developing more and more into brand-independent specialists, but to varying extents in the different European countries.

Captives are brand-related leasing companies, which offer leases in order to sell their own products. This is known as "sales financing". Captive leasing companies tend to be associated with major car manufacturers (General Motors, Mercedes-Benz, Ford), major truck manufacturers (Mercedes-Benz, Iveco, Volvo, Scania), photocopier manufacturers (Rank Xerox, Océ van der Grinten), computer manufacturers (IBM, Hewlett-Packard) and with construction machinery manufacturers (Caterpillar).

Apart from the sales financing element, leasing is a particularly useful tool for these suppliers since it allows them to offer the customer a complete service package (full-service lease). The customer is thereby guaranteed good maintenance and repair services, and the manufacturer is able to maintain an excellent relationship with the customer. In this way, the leased product offers a means of both managing overall commercial relationships and permanently monitoring customer satisfaction.

The third category, the independent leasing companies and intermediaries, consists of a wide range of (often quite small) leasing companies, most of which are involved in the leasing of cars, delivery vans and trucks. Many of these companies have a regional function and form part of a dealership. The leasing business is often a sideline of the main business (a car dealership, for example) and this business is often spun off when the portfolio becomes too large and starts putting too much strain on the vendor's own finances.

The 'intermediaries' category includes the brokers operating in the leasing market as brand-independent experts who advise companies on more complex investment issues with regard to means of production. In a sense, these brokers work as canvassers for new leasing contracts, which are then placed with banks for financing. In the eighties, brokers played a particularly active role on the computer market, leasing and selling mainframes.

The role of brokers has declined sharply in the wake of the shift of emphasis in the computer market to PCs and local networks. Moreover, some computer brokers suffered major problems in the late eighties when they took irresponsibly high residual value risks and went under as a result. This seriously undermined confidence in brokers in the leasing sector.

Vendor-leasing companies form a special category. These are joint ventures between general leasing companies and manufacturers or distributors of capital goods. This category is actually a hybrid of those discussed above, and is therefore not treated separately in statistical reports.

In Europe, the bank-affiliated leasing companies have by far the largest market share (74%). In the USA, however, the picture is different. Many US banks are regional operators and are not equipped to offer leasing. The position of independent suppliers such as GE Capital and AT&T Capital is therefore much stronger. These "non-banks" enjoy a dominant position in the American leasing market. They have developed a whole range of services which in Europe are offered by the banks.

There are also major differences in the type of product offered by the various categories of leasing. The bank subsidiaries in particular mainly offer finance leases, although a clear trend towards operating leases can be discerned. This development is also evident with other suppliers. Captives and vendor-leasing companies are the principal market players in operating and full-service leasing. Suppliers of capital goods were often already active in the second-hand market for their products before they ever took up leasing.

As a result they are often in a better position to realize residual value than the general leasing companies. Furthermore, for such products as computers, photocopiers and trucks, the supplier often attaches strategic value to having a strong hold on the second-hand market.

2.6 THE CONTENT OF THE LEASING PRODUCT

Leasing is a difficult concept to define. Essentially, it involves one party providing an economic good and another making use of it over a fixed period of time. This period is often related to the economic life of the commodity. Leasing is an alternative to purchasing or renting, but has features in common with both.

A company intending to invest in a particular means of production has a number of options. It may decide to purchase the means of production, in which case it acquires full ownership of it. As the investor, it will also have to determine how this investment is to be financed. It should also take account of the risks associated with ownership. One of these risks is the depreciation in the value of the goods, leaving a specific residual value at the end of the product's lifespan. It will have to calculate depreciation on the basis of the expected devaluation curve, as it forms part of the cost price of its product. A company that decides to purchase the means of production will expect to be able to use it productively over its economic lifespan. It will realize that there will be a risk involved in possible under-utilization, and will have to decide whether this risk is acceptable.

If the risk is not acceptable, for example, if the means of production are only required temporarily, the company might consider renting. By renting, the business obtains, as it were, rights of use for a certain period. The lessor/owner invests in the goods and is therefore responsible for financing them. The lessor also bears the economic risks associated with the investment. Other risks, such as possible loss of value through fire or theft, are borne by either the lessor or the lessee, as agreed between the parties.

We mentioned above that leasing has features in common with both purchasing and renting. It differs from purchasing in that property rights can only be acquired at a later date or not at all. Moreover, the duration of the lease contract does not necessarily have to be commensurate with the economic lifespan of the goods. Leasing therefore offers more options than purchasing. The user does not have to be the owner of the means of production, and therefore does not have to bear the risk of economic obsolescence. Nor does he have to commit himself to leasing the commodity for its entire economic lifespan; he may choose to do so for a shorter period.

This factor makes leasing similar to renting, which also involves obtaining the right of use for a set period. The difference between renting and leasing is that a rental agreement precludes the acquisition of property rights, whereas a leasing agreement allows for this at a given time. Another difference is the duration of the contract.

Rental periods vary greatly, from very short-term (day) rental to periods of many years. Leasing agreements, on the other hand, generally apply for several years. There is little economic sense in leasing over short periods, say for several months. Short-term rental contracts are more suitable in these circumstances.

2.7 FORMS OF THE PRODUCT

2.7.1 FINANCE AND OPERATING LEASES

There are two forms of leases: finance leases (which have more in common with bank loans) and operating leases (which have more in common with rental). These two categories hang on the issue of who actually bears the economic risk of the asset (i.e., the residual value risk). If it is the lessee (the user), it is a finance lease. If it is the lessor (the investor), then it is an operating lease.

It is important to distinguish here between legal ownership and economic ownership. Legal ownership refers to formal property titles, as recorded in official documents. Economic ownership revolves around the issue of who bears the risk of economic obsolescence. This is not necessarily the legal owner. In the case of finance leases, the lessee is in fact the economic owner, but as a rule in most countries the lessee will only gain legal ownership at the end of the contractual term. In the case of operating leases, the lessor has economic ownership by definition and is generally also the legal owner.

The definition of the concept "economic ownership" is determined by the degree to which residual value risk is actually incurred. This requires an assessment of the residual value in relation to the market value at any given time. A lease in which the residual value is reduced to a nominal sum does not qualify as an 'operating lease'. In this case the lessee, not the lessor, is the economic owner, and the agreement is still classed as a finance lease. To meet the defining criterion for an operating lease, the lessor should run a realistic price risk. The question as to what constitutes 'realistic risk' in such a case is partly determined by economic reality and by risk assessment.

When an option to purchase is fixed too low, the lessee is in fact economically obliged to make use of the option, because he will be forfeiting a price advantage if he fails to do so. Such a situation is termed an urgent option. However, by definition this remains a purchase *option* rather than a purchase *obligation*, as the latter implies transfer of the residual value risk to the lessee, which would make the product a finance lease.

The differences between finance leases and operating leases are fundamental. Generally speaking, a finance lease involves 100% financing of an asset with a contractual term related to the lifespan of the goods. To this extent, it has much in common with a bank loan.

An operating lease is more akin to rental. The lessor is the investor and bears the economic risks of the asset. He will therefore also enter the goods on the asset side of his balance-sheet. The lessee obtains full use of the goods during a period shorter than its economic life. He can decide at a given time to acquire legal title of ownership to the goods, subject to the conditions of the lease.

Although financial and operating leases are essentially different concepts, it is not always possible to distinguish them clearly from one another. The chalk lines on the field where leasing is played are not clearly marked, and they may even be redrawn in the course of the match. Furthermore, the playing field itself varies widely from country to country. We shall return to this point later.

A distinctive characteristic of leasing is the split between user's rights and proprietary rights. The philosophy behind the leasing product is that use is more important than title. On the other hand, there is no strict dividing line between ownership and usership, as is the case with rent. The renter has, in principle, no title to the goods as property, whereas a lessee may well have. In the long run, leasing offers the possibility of acquiring legal ownership of the goods. With rental, this is never the case. The features of financial and operating leases may be summarized as follows (box 2.4).

Box 2.4

FEATURES OF FINANCIAL AND OPERATIONAL LEASES

	Financial lease	**Operational lease**
Nature of contract	Form of financing	Form of rental
Who is the investor	The user/lessee	The lease company/lessor
Economic title	Lessee	Lessor
Legal title	Lessor	Lessor
Duration contract	Equal to economic lifespan	Shorter than economic lifespan
Entry on balance-sheet	Lessee	Lessor

2.7.2 *SERVICE LEASES*

In addition to the main products described above, there is also a form known as the "service lease". This involves an extension of the service provided by other services connected to the goods.

The best-known form of service leasing is the full-service car lease, where the leasing contract includes such services as repairs, maintenance, insurance, tyre replacements, road tax and fuel consumption. In this form of leasing, the right of use has been elaborated to its fullest extent. Another example of a sector offering service leasing is photocopiers. Photocopiers are usually rented or leased, and the charges are normally based on the number of copies made.

There are two different systems for service leasing, which vary according to the form in which the customer pays. Under the so-called *open calculation system*, the customer is charged on the basis of the actual amount of the services used. The customer periodically receives information on his usage and is billed accordingly. The period of the lease is therefore variable.

Under the *closed calculation system*, the customer is charged on the basis of a previously set price, regardless (within certain basic limits) of the volume of usage. The advantage to the customer of a closed system is that costs may be planned in advance with total accuracy. The disadvantage is that the customer may end up paying for services he does not use.

2.7.3 *PRODUCT FORMS AND LEGISLATION*

For the purposes of legislation, the product forms of leasing are defined largely in economic terms. One important criterion is clearly the extent to which economic risks are incurred, as discussed above. However, the concepts are not always clearly separated in objective terms, for example with regard to the question of who actually does bear the economic risk.

The subjective nature of the basis used in some definitions of leasing makes legislation difficult. Without unambiguous definition of terms, no readily applicable laws can be passed. There are three important areas which require clear legislation: (1) the annual accounts (in which balance sheet are the goods capitalized), (2) the fiscal aspect (who may apply depreciation for tax purposes, who can make use of any tax benefits, who pays VAT, etc), and (3) civil law (who holds the right of ownership, or the right to use the goods as collateral).

Given the ambigous nature of the operating lease concept, it is obvious enough that a strictly objective approach would be very difficult to achieve. As a consequence, the legislation and guidelines that exist for the various aspects are actually based on conventions and agreements.

These are the chalk lines that determine the size of the playing field and are drawn differently from country to country. We cannot go into detail about all the discrepancies here. Suffice it to say that in certain areas much effort is made on an international level to standardize the rules. In accountancy, for instance, there is an increasing acceptance of the Anglo-Saxon norms as laid down in the SSAP and FASB directives. These regulations include the so-called 90% criterion, which states that the present value of the terms of an operating lease may not exceed 90% of the initial investment.

2.8 MOTIVES FOR LEASING

What are the reasons for taking a lease, and what are the advantages and disadvantages of leasing? These are naturally key issues. To some extent, the motives can be derived directly from the product characteristics. We have seen that lease products come in many different shapes and sizes, so that no single, all-encompassing answer to this question is possible.

One important point is that the added value of the lease product has to be assessed against the background of the possible alternatives. Leasing is, after all, a hybrid between purchasing and rental, with features of both, so that in each case the customer will be asking himself whether he can gain the same product advantages through purchasing or renting.

Finally, the customer will always base his decision on his own specific needs. A business with ample funds available will not place as much importance on the liquidity advantages of leasing as a business with liquidity problems. So there are three aspects involved in the assessment of the added value of a lease: the specific features of the lease product, the assessment of the pros and cons compared to possible alternatives and the value which the individual customer places on certain product features.

Clearly, the evaluation of the product features will also be influenced by local and regional circumstances. The stage of development of the local economy, the quality of the banking system, and the sophistication of the legal system are some of the important factors.

In Eastern Europe, for instance, there is high demand for leasing, but the current legal system is not far enough developed to satisfy internationally-applied risk standards. As a result, international leasing companies treat the various Eastern European countries with caution. What, then, are the most important arguments in favor of leasing?

Liquidity

Leasing generally finances 100% of the investment, whilst bank loans often offer less favorable percentages of the capital (50% to 70%). This is one of the key advantages of leasing, and one which still attracts people to it. However, the more sophisticated the banking system becomes, the more this advantage loses its significance. If a debtor has good credentials, bankers are prepared to grant a 100% loan. For the less qualified debtors, however, this does not apply; in that case leasing does offer liquidity advantages. In addition, leasing can offer solutions tailored to the cash-flow pattern of a company. The leasing terms can, for instance, be adjusted to the specific cash flow of seasonal businesses or specific projects.

Flexibility

Leasing offers the opportunity to opt for shorter terms, sometimes with interim get-out clauses. This sort of flexibility is becoming increasingly important in an era in which businesses are having to become more adaptable. Obviously, flexibility comes at a price, and one which should be acceptable to the customer. But it is a relative concept with an entirely different meaning for an investment in real estate compared to an investment in a truck, for example.

Solvency/balance sheet ratios

Leasing offers an alternative to self-investment, whereby the goods do not have to be shown on the balance-sheet (off-balance solution). This makes it possible to reduce the balance sheet or to prevent it from being extended.

The balance sheet ratios therefore appear more favorable than in circumstances where the assets have to be stated. For some businesses, this is a decisive argument in favor of leasing, especially when performance is being assessed (partly) according to the quality of the financial ratios. For this factor to count, the investment concerned must, of course, be a large one. Leasing is therefore often favored for investments in real estate. For many US companies, keeping real estate investments off-balance is strict company policy.

This solvency argument is somewhat controversial. Some regard the off-balance aspect as a form of "balance-sheet cosmetics" which any critical financier would see through immediately. The art lies in distinguishing the authentic from the fake. A business which takes its own premises off the balance-sheet via a sale-and-lease back transaction will be regarded with suspicion. But if the company has already been renting the premises for some time, and subsequently purchases it and puts it on an operating lease basis via sale-and-leaseback, it is, economically speaking, still in the position of a tenant. Whether it will actually be considered as such by the auditor and the tax authorities will depend on the extent to which the lease satisfies the regulations in force.

Farming out residual value risk

Through leasing, the residual value risk of certain investments can be transferred to the lessor. This advantage is especially important for goods which are not only capital intensive, but where the investor cannot easily recover the residual value at the end of the lifespan. Examples are large computer systems (mainframes), expensive telephone installations, and photocopiers. This is also an important argument in the case of capital goods subject to rapid technological obsolescence.

The benefit becomes even greater when combined with the flexibility argument. In this case, the user has, via the interim get-out clause, the option to change his obsolete equipment for something more up to date. He carries no residual value risk and always has the use of state-of-the-art equipment.

Outsourcing

Leasing offers the possibility to contract out responsibility and (management) concern for the maintenance and management of capital goods. A well-known example of this is vehicle fleet management.

To manage and maintain the quality of the vehicle fleet costs a great deal of time and money, which a company might prefer to spend on other things. Leasing companies have the know-how and expertise to take over these tasks from the customer. Usually, the customer company obtains a better service at a lower price than it would get by performing the tasks in question itself.

Outsourcing is becoming an increasingly important aspect of the leasing industry. Companies are becoming more and more willing to contract out services if they perceive advantages from doing so. The demand for this form of service provision is therefore growing, and leasing companies are continuously offering new applications in this area. A few years ago, not many transport companies would have been interested in a full-service vehicle lease. In-house maintenance of the vehicle fleet was considered part of the core business.

Now, attitudes have changed dramatically. In the haulage business, actual physical transport is increasingly being sub-contracted. To have an in-house vehicle fleet and take care of its maintenance is increasingly less suited to the present management style in this industry.

Convenience

Leasing can also be a means of realizing convenience aspects. The driver of a leased car does not have to worry about maintenance, receives substitute transport if the car is in for servicing or repair, fills up on gas with the lease company's fuel card, does not have to keep administrative records or produce receipts in order to claim expenses. Such advantages may be an important reason for the user to consider leasing. However, it is no exception from the ancient rule that 'there ain't no such thing as a free lunch'.

Budgeting

Leasing can contribute to improved control over business costs, since fluctuations can be eliminated through fixed lease terms. The user knows exactly where he stands; he can, as it were, buy security with leasing.

Tax advantages

Sometimes tax advantages are available from taking a lease which are difficult or impossible to obtain otherwise. One example here is the tax investment premium which applies or used to apply in some countries (tax credit). Sometimes, companies make insufficient profit to enjoy this tax benefit to its fullest extent. Here, leasing can make it possible to still claim most of it. There are also advantages in cross-border leases, which can allow a lessee in country A to profit from the tax advantages in country B. These benefits were more widely available some years ago; the tax authorities have now taken more of a hand in restricting the possibilities in this area. However, they are still an advantage of leasing at present.

Chapter 3 The market strategy aspects of leasing

3.1 *INTRODUCTION*

This chapter discusses how leasing companies can position themselves on the market and what the strategic considerations are here. Market strategy has been described above as the positioning of a business in the market. The choices to be made here revolve around the type of products and services a company wants to deploy on the market. What, then, is the best way to address these issues in the leasing sector?

Lease products cater for a wide variety of demands. In the early days of leasing, these demands traditionally revolved around finding solutions to financial problems. One well-known example here is the US manufacturer United Shoe Machinery Corporation: in the 19th century, the company discovered that there was a great deal of demand for its machines - but that many potential customers could not afford them. Sales could be given a major boost by renting out the machines. This is how the phenomenon of sales financing arose.

In the course of time, opportunities for obtaining finance through banks have opened up tremendously, so that the customer is no longer dependent on the supplier to finance his investment. Sales financing is still used a great deal today, but for different reasons. The overriding factor today is the strategic importance of sales financing to the supplier. By providing finance, he can offer the customer a total solution to his investment needs; he may also be able to provide supplementary services such as servicing and maintenance.

At the same time, he is in a good position to capture replacement investments when the time comes, and might even be able to influence the timing of the replacement. Sales financing also offers the supplier the opportunity to influence the second-hand market, and thus generate additional revenue from re-marketing.

When designing a market strategy in this sector, the extreme wide range of motives for leasing on both sides of the lessee/lessor fence should always be borne in mind. Naturally, these motives will also change over time, so that the strategy has to be updated continuously.

It would not make a great deal of sense to analyze market strategy for leasing from a general point of view. The product has a wide range of applications which diverge so widely that the leasing market may, in fact, be regarded as a large number of small, individual submarkets. One of the strategic choices a leasing company has to make is the choice between the various positions on the various markets (or submarkets). We will begin our strategic analysis with this aspect.

The next point concerns the value or, if you like, the added value that a plans to offer in the (sub)market. By "value", we understand in this case the importance a product or service has for the consumer. What customer need does the product fulfill, and what benefits does the product offer compared to competing products? These issues will be discussed in section 3.3.

The third aspect is the direction in which the company wants to develop. This will affect the actual strategic choices to be made. These choices should be made against the background of a critical evaluation of the company's current strengths and weaknesses and a clear conception of the market and the future. The most important issue is the choice of the areas in which the business wants to **excel** in the future, and the resources it would like to invest to achieve this objective. These issues will be explored in section 3.4.

Examining market strategy issues in this order allows us to analyze the problems systematically. However, they do not necessarily have to be approached in this order in practice; indeed, the above sequence would not be entirely logical in the real world.

In practice, the point of departure is often the formulation of a "corporate mission" which is then translated into concrete strategic actions. The corporate mission reflects the principal objectives of the company and how it hopes to realize them. These objectives are then translated into a corporate strategy for a specific period, which is evaluated and, if necessary, adjusted at intervals of no more than a year. The discussion below, however, is more concerned with a general analysis of market strategy issues in the leasing market.

3.2 STRATEGIC POSITIONING IN THE LEASING MARKET

The first feature of the market strategy of a leasing company that we are going to consider is its position in the leasing market. This position is determined by three factors: the product offering, distribution and the customer categories.

3.2.1 THE PRODUCT OFFERING

Offerings in the leasing sector may be classed according to two features: the nature of the product (finance lease, operating lease, service lease) and the nature of the goods (moveable assets, real estate and intangible assets). These three categories represent widely divergent products. Moveable assets may also be further sub-divided into rolling and non-rolling stock, because of the size of the two market segments concerned. The category of intangible assets has been included because it is very interesting from a strategic point of view, however, it is currently of little significance on the market.

3.2.2 THE DISTRIBUTION STRUCTURE

The distribution structure may be typified on the one hand by the nature of the distribution channel (banks, captives and independents) and, on the other hand, in terms of geographic scope. The "independents" category includes independent general leasing companies as well as dealers and brokers. It is probably the largest in terms of the number of companies, particularly in view of the large number of suppliers among automobile and truck dealers.

However, there is little information available on this category. The leasing business is often a marginal activity, regarded as a supporting service to enhance sales of the main products. Due to this lack of information, we will not spend much time discussing this category.

3.2.3 THE CUSTOMER CATEGORIES

The type of customer is decided by the following features: private individuals versus companies, national versus international customers, the industry in which the corporate customer operates and the size of the company. The previous chapter gives the figures for the various customer categories. These indicate that the private segment is growing, but is still of little significance in the market as a whole. We will therefore disregard this customer group and focus entirely on the corporate market.

The criterion of company size will only be considered for the national market: this market includes local suppliers for local customers, many of which are small or medium-sized businesses. For the international market, this distinction is hardly relevant. The above three criteria - product offering, distribution structure, customer categories - make it possible to typify the strategic position of leasing companies.

It is, in effect, a way of indicating where a company may be found. So far, we have no information as to why a company takes up a certain position. Under each of the three aspects, leasing companies almost always occupy several positions. General leasing companies are active in the largest number of fields. As stated above, in Europe these are almost always banks. Captives are usually more specialized. They confine themselves to a specific type of goods (their own products) and often also have narrowly defined geographic markets. They usually confine themselves to the customer category that buys their core product.

Those companies with the most restricted activities are the local and regional suppliers, not only because of the geographic limitations of the market but also because of the limited range of products offered. These suppliers often have only limited know-how and experience of the leasing field, because to them leasing is usually just a sideline. They are often suppliers of finance leases. Local suppliers hoping to develop their leasing activities further opt for collaboration with a general leasing company or make use of the leasing facilities offered by a captive company.

The three above-mentioned structural characteristics are obviously closely interrelated. Providing service to an international customer requires an international distribution channel and a product which can be sold internationally, i.e. it requires an international leasing company. However, this does not necessarily mean that such companies cannot also be active locally - in fact, they usually are.

One strategic issue here is whether an international leasing company should be just as active on the local market as a local supplier. The answer will depend on the added value a leasing company can offer in the two market segments, and the extent to which they can be combined.

There are still very few international leasing companies in Europe, as a result of the different legislation, currencies, languages and cultures in the various European countries. Clearly, in view of the advances in European unification, the strategy of an increasing number of leasing companies will be focusing on Europe.

3.3 THE VALUE OF THE LEASE PRODUCT

After a company's market positioning has been determined, the question then arises of how much value is created with the lease product. As mentioned above, by "value" we understand the importance of the lease product to the customer. Our next question must therefore be: what customer need does the product meet?

By formulating the question in this way, we place the customer at the center of attention. It has already been stated that a product-based approach makes little marketing sense today. Changes in the market are happening so fast that a product-oriented approach will almost always be behind the times. Knowledge of the nature of customer requirements now offers the only basis for developing a sound strategy. It is also the only way to predict and anticipate future market developments.

The value of the lease product can be determined by the motives for taking lease, as described in chapter 2 above. The following motives were discussed: liquidity, flexibility, solvency, farming out residual value risk, outsourcing, convenience, budgeting and tax advantages. These motives indicate why a customer might make use of leasing. From this starting point, we can infer the type of solutions the lease product offers the customer.

When we look at the benefits from this point of view, the following problem areas emerge: finance problems (e.g., making funds available for investments), cash flow problems (providing enough liquidity to guarantee an uninterrupted flow of payment streams), cost problems (controlling and lowering company costs as much as possible), risk problems (whether the future book values of assets can be realized or not), control and management problems (problems flowing from the management and maintenance of certain assets or groups of assets - such as vehicle fleets).

These five problem areas indicate the kind of solutions offered by leasing. The next question to be examined is the extent to which leasing offers better or more cost-efficient solutions than alternative products. We will examine this issue in more detail for each of the problem areas.

3.3.1 *SOLUTIONS FOR FINANCING PROBLEMS*

Whether leasing is the most appropriate solution to a financing problem depends on a number of factors.

It is important, for example, to know the other options, if any, that are available to a customer seeking to finance an investment. One alternative to leasing, for instance, would be a medium-term loan. However, banks have doled out such support for several decades with a very tight fist. Substantial long-term loans were simply not granted. Only very healthiest companies were eligible. Leasing therefore offered a unique advantage for companies who would not be eligible for major bank loans.

In most European countries, the banking system is now well developed and there is a wide choice of financing products. The time when leasing could offer a unique financing solution has gone. Today's customer will be in a position to weigh up the benefits of leasing against the option of a bank loan. The following factors play a role in this choice: the quality of the customer, the nature of the goods, the price and speed (convenience).

The quality of the customer

The higher the quality of the customer, the more options he will be offered at the bank. In the case of very sound companies, the security value of the asset to be financed is less important, because banks will be prepared to grant unsecured credit up to a certain point. Consequently, the value of leasing increases as the security value of the asset concerned becomes a more important factor in granting credit. This last aspect will apply to customers in a somewhat higher risk category, or customers for whom the size of the investment requires good, asset-backed collateral.

The nature of the goods

The security value is also of course related to the nature of the goods. The added value of leasing is greatest for standard goods for which there is an active second-hand market. A more general rule is that the added value of the leasing company is strongly determined by the extent to which it is able to manage residual value risks.

Specialization according to categories of goods is becoming increasingly significant, and re-marketing also appears to be growing increasingly international in character.

The price

In choosing between different financing alternatives, price obviously plays an important role. For a proper price comparison, it is important to have equivalent products, which can lead to problems in the case of leasing. We will elaborate on this in more detail in section 3.3.3.

Speed and convenience

Aspects such as speed and convenience also play a role in the customer's decision-making process. With leasing, a contract has to be drawn up each time, which will be considered a hindrance in some cases. This applies not only to the customer, but also to the account manager of the bank, who is experienced in granting bank loans and might therefore be more inclined to offer a bank loan rather than a lease. In other cases, the aspects of speed and convenience will operate in favor of leasing.

A dealer offering his customer an all-inclusive leasing offer when he purchases a motor vehicle assists the customer quickly and simply in solving his financing problem. If the application can be made without red tape and the price tag is acceptable, the customer will probably make his decision quickly. It appears that this form of sales financing will grow strongly in the future.

3.3.2 SOLUTIONS FOR CASH FLOW PROBLEMS

The added value of leasing here lies in matching incoming and outgoing cash streams. The amounts of the installments are adjusted over the term of the contract to match fluctuations in income. This principle is applied to companies where business is seasonal or to projects in which cash flow is irregular, and is known as the pay-as-you-earn principle.

These are, then, tailor-made solutions which could conceivably have been achieved by other means, but where the leasing solution is often related to specific knowledge of exploiting certain assets or specialist expertise in a specific industry. From this point of view, leasing sometimes offers an advantage over the non-specialized bank products. It should also be mentioned here that leasing often offers more liquidity than a bank loan.

3.3.3 SOLUTIONS FOR COST PROBLEMS

Does leasing offer cost advantages over a bank loan? For a proper comparison, a pure finance lease should be compared to a bank loan, because otherwise other value elements would have to be taken into consideration which could interfere with the comparison. Price differences may stem from the following factors: cost of funding, margins and taxation differences.

Cost of funding

There may be differences in funding costs between a leasing company and a bank. These differences will, of course, not arise where the leasing company and the bank belong to the same organization. In Europe this is often the case, as 75% of leasing companies are allied to banks. Banks and leasing companies will therefore often have the same level of funding costs, so that no cost advantages can be expected here. In the case of leasing companies which are not allied to banks, the price difference will often be to the disadvantage of leasing, because the funding costs of these leasing companies are generally higher.

Margin

This refers to the mark-up over and above funding costs. Leasing is, on the whole, more labor-intensive because of the documentation needed. Standardization is much further advanced with bank loans than with leasing, and, moreover, sales of bank loans are much higher. This means that cost advantages will lie with bank loans than with leases, and the margins on leases will therefore usually be higher than those on bank loans. In practice, however, it is often difficult to trace this price difference, for instance when leasing offers more liquidity than a bank loan. The products are then no longer identical, so that the comparison is no longer valid.

Taxation differences

Sometimes cost differences occur for fiscal reasons, as was the case for instance with the tax credits or deferment in various countries in the past. Leasing sometimes offers advantages in these cases which could not have been obtained with a loan. In fact, we are no longer talking of a pure leasing advantage here, since leasing then becomes an instrument for the realization of tax benefits. In the Netherlands, this situation occurred in the days of the WIR (Wet op de InvesteringsRekening - law governing investment calculation). In the USA, the TRAC lease (Terminal Rental Adjustment Clause Lease) is based on it. More generally, it should also be mentioned that the international market for cross-border leasing is almost completely geared to obtaining tax advantages.

3.3.4 SOLVING RISK PROBLEMS

Solving risk problems in this context refers principally to solving residual value problems. One of the most typical features of the leasing product is that it offers outstanding opportunities for farming out residual value risks. In the case of bank financing, this element is absent.

The value of the lease product has to be assessed against the background of the alternative in which the entrepreneur bears the risk himself, as well as the price which he has to pay to transfer it to a third party. Considerations of corporate policy often play an important role here, for example the policy of not bearing the risks in real estate. For US companies this is often a reason to rent or lease immovables. Balance sheet considerations also come into this category. The desire to keep certain investments off the balance sheet is, in fact, the accountant's version of a policy aimed at farming out residual value risks or aiming for flexibility with regard to certain investments.

Another argument in favor of taking a lease may be that the leasing companies can manage the residual value risks better than the entrepreneur/user. This argument belongs in the category of core business considerations, where a company has to decide what activities will give it the highest returns. It may be assumed that a leasing company specializing in leasing heavy goods vehicles will have better remarketing results than a non-specialist. In this case, the leasing company contributes a special skill which the banks do not have. We have already mentioned above that this specialization in specific categories of goods is becoming an increasingly important factor in the leasing industry.

The management of residual value risks demands specific skills which, furthermore, can only be exercised if the leasing company also has access to the second-hand market. In some cases the second-hand market is largely controlled by the manufacturers or suppliers, examples here are photocopiers and large computer systems. On these markets, it is virtually impossible for third parties to occupy justifiable risk positions, as the influence of captives is so high.

3.3.5 SOLUTIONS FOR CONTROL AND MANAGEMENT PROBLEMS

Leasing is not only confined to solving financing and investment problems, but also includes services involving the control and management of assets. In actual fact, this service provision flows logically from the services for managing residual value risks described above. It may be regarded as a further development of know-how and expertise in asset management.

Here too, the leasing company must be able to perform better in these areas than the customer itself. Specialist leasing companies will certainly be able to demonstrate their added value in the case of assets which typically do not form part of the core business of the customer company.

The borderlines between what is and what is not core business are, however, constantly shifting. A good example is the transport sector, in which, until a short time ago, the control and management of one's own vehicle fleet was deemed to be part of the core business. However, in the face of ever-declining returns on actual physical transportation, many transport companies have now turned to subcontracting this part of their activities. As a result, the investment and control of vehicle fleets now appears in an entirely new light. Instead of carrying out transportation services themselves, these businesses have become arrangers of transport services. The transport company has developed into a provider of logistics services, farming out a substantial proportion of transportation services instead of performing them in-house. This new attitude means that it is no longer appropriate to invest in vehicle fleets yourself, but more sensible to leave this to third parties.

These third parties are often small transport companies which do not have the in-house maintenance services and facilities that the larger players of the past often did. Leasing companies have specialized in the management and maintenance of vehicle fleets, and are as a rule able to do this better and more economically than the small transportation companies. Furthermore, this specialism among leasing companies is still in full swing. This phenomenon is related to the development and application of up-to-date information systems, which supply the company with all the information needed to ensure efficient use of means of transport.

Nowadays, information is no longer just a supporting tool in business, it has increasingly become a valuable asset in its own right. As a result of investments in information technology, thus contributing to improving management efficiency and the effectiveness, the added value of the lease product is increased more and more. At the same time, however, the question arises of an important change in the nature of the service provided by leasing.

It will have become clear from the above that leasing is undergoing a major development at the moment. The original value of the product, which lay mainly in offering financing solutions, is shifting increasingly towards the provision of solutions for investment in, control of and management of assets. The information technology element will play an increasing role in this. The clear implication is that a new type of leasing company will emerge which will have to satisfy new and different demands.

3.4 STRATEGIC CHOICES

When we talk about a marketing oriented approach to the leasing market, we are not talking about offering products, but about offering solutions to customers. It is therefore obvious that market strategy issues should also be formulated in these terms. Market strategy thus revolves around the issue of which problems should be solved for which customers.

First of all, a clear insight should be gained into the company's good qualities at any given point in time. A popular approach here is strengths / weaknesses analysis, often in combination with an analysis of the opportunities and threats in the market. These analyses provide useful information for strategic management, but they are not always applied properly in practice. They are sometimes little more than part of a regular annual ritual, in which little in the way of real critical analysis of the company's market position can be seen. The challenge to investigate the current and future demands of the customer in more depth is often lacking.

A more challenging approach would be the following. If the customer requests tailor-made solutions, why not make it the company's objective to be able to offer each customer a tailor-made solution? This solution would also have to be better and more attractive than that offered by the competition.

We will investigate below what is required in order to realize this objective, at the same time gaining insights into the most important strategic choices. The most important assets in fulfilling the formulated objective are know-how and information technology. By "know-how", we mean in this context all information regarding the wishes of the customer as well as the options for satisfying these wishes. Information technology enables us to realize the latter part of this effectively and efficiently on a large scale.

The function of modern information technology is absolutely essential. It is probably the single most important reason for the swing towards customer-centered thinking. Information technology is important in the following areas: capturing individual customer needs, offering support when advising customers, computerization of business processes, producing relevant customer information and producing relevant management information.

Information technology will supply systems for all these aspects which will make it possible to satisfy a wide range of customer requirements on an increasingly large scale. The choice of which direction a company will take with regard to IT is therefore an important aspect of strategic management.

Information systems are expensive, and developments in the market are extremely rapid. In order to build competitive advantages in this area sufficient scale advantages will be needed, since otherwise it will be impossible to recoup the costs within a reasonable time. But the infrastructure needed for these systems is another reason why sufficient scale is required.

3.5 MARKET SEGMENTS

Market volume thus becomes an important aspect of our strategic considerations. After all, we are seeing a development in which unique, tailor-made products are ever more rapidly becoming a commodity. The distinctive character of the products is declining, and price competition is growing. Cost-effectiveness is therefore becoming increasingly important. For the development of market volume, the distinction between the following three segments is important: the retail segment, the middle segment and the corporate segment.

Retail segment

The retail segment is that part of the market which is characterized by standardized mass production and in which personal customer relationships play a less important role. It includes private individuals as well as companies, and the sale of financing products is increasingly taking place through electronic media. A great deal of the business transactions are impersonal, and the customer will allow his choice to be strongly determined by aspects such as price, speed, reliability and existing (traditional) customer loyalty.

Middle segment

The middle segment consists of companies in which some form of personal contact with the customer is essential for the business relationship. Information technology also plays an important role here in the sale of lease products, but customers have to be advised individually in order to arrive at the desired tailor-made solution.

The customer in this segment will not only consider such aspects as price and speed, but will also keep a keen watch on the quality of the service and advice provided, as well as the level of commitment he gets from the leasing company.

Corporate segment

The corporate segment is made up of large companies, both listed and unlisted. These companies purchase products in large volumes, including standardized products (such as vehicle fleet management). But they also require specific solutions requiring a high level of specialist professional know-how.

Leasing solutions and corporate finance issues go hand in hand here, and aspects of international taxation also play an important role. In this segment, personal relationships and the input of high-quality expertise are crucial. It is also very much a global market; the large international vendors maintain contacts with customers all over the world.

The retail market is the most important for the development of market volume. The development of information technology enables this mass market to be served on a large scale at relatively low cost. Linking information networks with distribution networks will be vital here. The information networks take care of all aspects of data processing and electronic support functions; the distribution networks determine the way in which contacts with customers are maintained.

Modern information technology is creating many new options in the area of distribution. In addition to the existing distribution channels such as banks and suppliers, many other points of sale can be used to sell leasing products.

In the future, every point of sale will also be a potential leasing point. Retail marketing will therefore become an important future area for the leasing sector and may even provide the platform for a new generation of retail leasing specialists.

In this context, it is also interesting to look at how large US leasing companies operate in the retail market. Companies such as The Associates, CE Capital and the CIT Group are active on the credit card market as well as the private finance market and the small-ticket leasing market. These companies have developed special strengths in the area of controlling and managing large payment and information flows, and it is evident that a combined package of activities on the retail market can lead to important synergy advantages. There are also significant synergy advantages in the area of distribution: all these companies have an extensive network of offices in the USA which can be used for marketing various products.

The cost of information will cease to cramp growth in the retail market of the future. Technologically speaking, the possibilities for expansion are endless; in practice, however, there are other growth-restricting factors, for example the problems of providing adequate management of customer contacts and risk management. However, sophisticated information technology becomes, personal customer contacts will not be completely superseded by electronic transactions.

After all, before a lease contract is concluded both the debtor and the goods/residual value risk will be assessed, so personal contact with the customer needs to be maintained in one way or another. This personal contact, however, does not have to be effected by the leasing company itself. It may also be channeled through the point of sale: the bank, the dealer or the retailer. However, a distribution network will clearly still be needed for penetration of the retail market, despite the possibilities of the electronic age. Holding good distribution positions on the retail market offers important strategic advantages, the importance of which cannot be overestimated. In this connection, we can compare the situation of other segments in the retail market, such as clothing, food, the DIY trade etc., in which this development has been going on over a far longer period. It appears that optimum exploitation of distribution channels will thus become an important factor in achieving improved returns.

A leasing company which has established a good position on the retail market will also apply this position to the middle segment, since doing so offers important synergies in terms of return on distribution. Operating in the middle segment does, however, require a greater degree of specialization, on both the finance and the goods side.

There is a clear difference from the retail market here. In the middle segment, there is increasing demand for specialization in such areas as cars, trucks, computers, photocopiers etc. This specialization can be provided by experts from the industry, who can offer the company the solutions required.

As a rule, the specialization is of such an independent nature that suppliers operate on the market from separate, specialized leasing companies. This does not, however, detract from the fact that there are definitely synergy advantages to be obtained in the retail segment. The special skill in managing flows of money and information, the key characteristic of the retail segment, will thus be extended to include expertise related to managing and controlling vehicle fleets, for example.

In principle, these types of service can be extended almost indefinitely. A business specializing in the area of vehicle fleet management could also develop expertise in logistics services. Customer requests, for example, might lead to a further expansion of service provision in that direction. This is what happened at the US company Ryder, the largest truck leasing company in the world. As well as leasing trucks and delivery vans, they have, over the years, also developed a substantial transport company, which now, for example, provides transportation in the USA for around 2.6 million motor cars per year from the factory gates to the station or harbor. This activity has also been further developed into the provision of pure logistics services, in which Ryder acts only as the organizer of transportation activities.

This example demonstrates just how far the frontiers of the leasing industry can be pushed back.

The corporate segment appears to be pretty much a separate part of the market, in which specialization takes place on an independent scale, sometimes but not always in combination with corporate banking. There are many international suppliers who focus on this segment almost exclusively, especially in the segments of airplanes, ships and rolling stock.

But there are other variants as well; leasing activities which are inseparable from banking activities, as well as suppliers who are active in all the above-mentioned segments. In principle, there are synergies here too (such as utilizing the available expertise in the field of leasing) but these are less significant in practice.

We can conclude from the above that realizing market volume will be an important strategic factor for leasing companies in the future. This will be less the case in the corporate segment, where the reputation of the supplier is a very real factor and the market will thus be dominated by large, well-known suppliers.

The most important strategic choices may be summarized as follows:

- Determining the type of leasing service provision in which the company would like to be strong. This especially concerns the question of whether to choose a large range with high volume or a small range which is specialized to a great extent.
- The choice between the above mentioned segments.
- The choice of geographic scope, especially the choice between national and international leasing.
- The choice of information strategy.
- The choice of distribution strategy.

Probably the most essential quality by which the leasing company can gain competitive differentiation is the further development of core competence. This applies not only to the professional know-how and expertise required to offer certain services, but also to aspects such as creativity, originality and innovativeness. It involves all those factors which determine why a business is capable of excelling in a certain area. Setting the direction for this development is possibly the single most important factor in the strategy of any leasing company.

Chapter 4 Marketing and the European leasing industry: a survey

4.1 INTRODUCTION

It's no news to even the most casual observer of the financial services industry that these are exciting and challenging times for financial institutions. The pace of change and the growing complexity around are truly breathtaking. The information revolution, globalization, increasing buying sophistication and significant demographic changes are driving forces behind these changes. For marketers, the implications are far-reaching: an exponential growth in information availability and use, new parts of the globe opening up, rapidly fragmenting demand, a proliferation of distibution channels, shortened product, project and process life cycles, and intensified, often price-based competition.

These trends are all the more challenging because many companies are emerging from a period dominated by cost-cutting, downsizing or delayering. In other words: after a prolonged period of internal focus, companies must again concentrate on external issues, and put marketing at the top of their agenda. This presents a major challenge to the financial services industry, where marketing skills are all but "state-off-the-art". The leasing industry is no exception.

In this chapter, we will touch on the following issues: the four development stages of business marketing, excellence in business marketing, the methodology and the main results of a survey conducted among European leasing companies and the leasing industry's marketing challenge.

4.2 THE FOUR DEVELOPMENT STAGES OF BUSINESS MARKETING

The focus of this chapter is on the wholesale side of leasing. Business marketing - also known as "industrial marketing" or "business-to-business marketing" - is the marketing of products and/or services for transformation or "consumption" by businesses. Business marketing obviously differs from consumer marketing in several respects: (1) the number of the customers it targets, (2) the nature of the customers it targets, and (3) the complexity of the decision-making processes business marketers go through with their customers.

Business marketing specialists operate in an environment where the industry structure determines their actions, and where price and production costs are the crucial levers. The main thrust of the marketing efforts of consumer and business marketing specialists does show some similarities, such as the importance of channel management and of product development. However, there are also notable differences between the two, such as: (1) the predominance of the sales function, (2) the importance of pricing tactics, and (3) the need for partnerships with customers in business marketing.

Business marketing has developed over time. We can identify four main eras of business marketing: the sales era (from World War II through the 50s), the product/service era (the 60s until the late 70s), the customer era (the early 80s until the mid 90s) and the needs-driven era (starting in the mid 90s). Each era has different driving forces, requires different key marketing skills and is characterized by different marketing hallmarks.

The sales era was a time of booming primary demand: the industrial base expanded rapidly and companies like IBM set the standards for the sales function that we still apply today. It also witnessed the development of the now traditional 4 Ps of the marketing mix - Price, Product, Promotion and Place. The 4 Ps framework had several advantages. It was easy to apply, served as a powerful communication tool, and was an effective instrument for solving marketing-related problems.

In those days, the 4 Ps framework was first and foremost a consumer marketing tool. Business marketing at that time was in essence synonymous with knowing "How to win friends and influence people". When business marketers used the 4 Ps model, they generally focused on the two core Ps, i.e. Pricing and Product.

As the level of (mainly domestic) - competition increased in the 1960s and 1970s, new marketing tools were needed. Brand marketing came into fashion. Marketing executives were generally "product champions" who knew a great deal about the products they sold. P for Packaging became increasingly important in this era, especially for industrial and retail companies. In financial services, Packaging stands for adding value beyond the basic product by providing certain additional services. Differentiation became a way to deal with the fragmentation of markets and their segments.

The growing importance of market research was the most prominent feature of the next era, the "customer era". Market research became an important competitive medium as customer markets became increasingly fragmented and growth in primary demand slowed, resulting in a more competitive playing field.

Knowledge about the "Position" of a company in its own industry, and about the relationship between it and its customers, became an important strategic asset. Companies used competitive analyses to determine their market position vis-à-vis their competitors, and market analyses to establish their position vis-à-vis their existing and prospective customers. Strategic marketing became an important topic: understanding and responding to customer buying behavior using such strategies as demographic segmentation.

The last era, the "needs-driven era", has only just started and is marked by an often flat primary demand, rising customer sophistication, cut-throat competition, an explosive growth in the amount of information available and used, and an increasing number of alliances/-partnerships, some of them across borders.

The essence of business marketing in this environment today consists of creating and developing new markets and/or businesses, sometimes with partners. The main components of this process include (1) identifying unfulfilled customer needs, (2) being proactive in pricing and product development strategies and (3) managing marketing information efficiently and effectively.

The people working for the companies in question are responsible for the breadth, depth and quality of customer relationships. This adds two more Ps to the 6 Ps of the third business marketing era: Partners and People.

4.3 ELEMENTS OF EXCELLENCE

Era four-type companies in the financial services industry, such as Goldman Sachs and Merrill Lynch, provide us with best-practice examples in the field of business marketing skills. In essence, frontrunners like these know how to add and maximize value. Their focus is not only on getting the aforementioned marketing basics - the 8 Ps

- right, but also on the attributes that drive customer choice, knowing how to limit costs and how to innovate extensively:

- Best-practice business marketing specialists are dyed-in-the-wool customer marketers. They have an intimate knowledge of the attributes that drive customer choice and they induce changes to affect the customer's choice. For example, they advertise and promote product messages as well as relevant corporate messages in a highly targeted manner. They have strong pricing skills and know how to manage these skills, both strategically (controlling price levels, setting value-based prices) and tactically (offering discounts). Best-practice marketers determine which customers or prospective customers are attractive, when and why. Then they choose which ones to serve, and vary the mix as circumstances change.

- Second, successful business marketers keep their costs low for the value they choose to provide. They decide where to pitch the value they deliver to customers by consciously considering their current and potential cost position and their unique assets and skills. Successful business marketers do not just cut costs in-house, but also use non-traditional, marketing-oriented cost-reduction tools, such as alliances or partnerships with customers.

- Third, successful business marketing specialists shape the industries they compete in. This requires aggressive innovation. Whenever possible, it also involves global scope - which means building an understanding of international customers - and building a flexible and focused skills-based organization capable of continuous improvement. The industry shaper understands how his industry is structured and what marketing options and channels will make it most profitable. He takes a broad view of his customer and of the products or markets that make up his competitive arena.

Needless to say, many companies still have a long way to go before they reach this high skill level. Many still focus on price to influence customer choices, and operate at the mercy of the demand flow. These companies merely react to changes in the industry, and define their business by the product they make. They look no further than selling and sales support, continue to hold customers at arm's length, rarely innovate, and generate only marginal revenue from new products. They confine themselves to building strength in domestic markets only, wait for others to invent new channels, continue to rely exclusively on their own business systems, and ignore the opportunities provided by alliances and partnerships. They will not be competitive enough for tomorrow's markets.

In general, the leasing industry is still a long way from marketing excellence. Most leasing companies are still in the second era, focused on professionalizing their basic product tailoring and their customer classification skills. Their aim is to become excellent sellers of excellent financial products and services. Most leasing companies are product-oriented instead of customer-oriented: they focus on their own needs, the needs of the seller.

Learning how to create strategies aimed at understanding and adding value to customers is a key issue. Leasing companies have to develop focused strategies to identify, segment and exploit customer needs which could offer promising potential. Formulating such strategies is a tough job, implementing them may be even tougher. Implementing a focused strategy means choosing between different alternatives that are often all attractive, for example selling the same product with two different technologies / distribution strategies to different customer segments which are both profitable. Commitment to a choice is a key success factor here, given the inherent shortage of financial and / or managerial resources.

Some financial companies such as Citicorp and NatWest excel in making these choices. What distinguishes them from the ruck? First, they understand and use need-based market segmentation principles. Second, they know how to monitor customers' explicit and implicit desires and wants as well as competitive activity. They possess a corporate culture where marketing plays a key role, and use concepts providing unique value to the customer. In short: they have a strong customer orientation.

4.4 METHODOLOGY OF THE SURVEY

The key to attaining competitive advantage is satisfying the explicit and implicit needs of the customer. Most leasing companies have also found themselves faced with the need for greater cost control. These two major pressures can easily end up in conflict: on the one hand, there is the externally focused need to improve customer orientation and tailor market offerings closely to customer requirements.

On the other hand, there is the internal need to improve operating efficiency by reducing staff while simplifying and standardizing core processes. Resolving the dilemma, and achieving a balance between "looking out" and "looking in", is one of the key challenges for leasing companies for the remainder of the 1990s.

Against this backdrop, our survey was conceived as a way of highlighting the major changes occurring in the market place and also identifying the approaches and strategies the more successful firms are adopting to cope with, and profit from, such changes.

The data was collected during the summer of 1995. More than one hundred executives (118) from leasing companies in seven European countries (the Netherlands, Italy, the United Kingdom, Spain, France, Germany and Sweden) completed a detailed questionnaire. We received information about leasing products, market segments in the leasing industry, the marketing organization of and processes within leasing companies, the marketing mix used, and future trends in the industry.

The response to our questionnaire was high in Italy, the Netherlands and the UK, while German, Spanish and French leasing companies seemed reluctant to participate. Almost all the Swedish leasing companies participated, but as a group, they represent only a small proportion of the sample.

Box 4.1 *(Source: McKinsey&Company)*

LOCATION OF COMPANY, %	
Germany	11%
UK	14%
Netherlands	14%
Italy	38%
Sweden	7%
Spain	8%
France	8%
100% = 118 companies	

Roughly one third of the 118 respondents were based in Italy, one third in the UK and the Netherlands, and one third in Sweden, Spain, France and Germany. Three quarters of the respondents were subsidiaries of banks, almost one in five were captive companies, while only 5 percent were independent.

Box 4.2 *(Source: McKinsey&Company)*

STATUS OF THE COMPANY, %	
Subsidiary of a bank	74%
Captive	18%
Independent	5%
Other	3%
100% = 118 companies	

In terms of portfolio structure, the overwhelming majority were equipment lessors. The major product areas in the portfolio were machinery and industrial equipment, computers and business machines, and vehicles such as cars, trucks and trailers.

Box 4.3 *(Source: McKinsey&Company)*

PORTFOLIO BUILD-UP EQUIPMENT, %	
I. Real estate	18%
II. Equipment	82%
- machinery & industrial equipment (34%)	
- cars (21%)	
- computers & business machines (19%)	
- trucks & trailers (14%)	
- aircraft (4%)	
- railway rolling stock (2%)	
- ships (1%)	
- other (5%)	
100% = 108 companies	

Although financial leasing still accounts for most of the sales, operating leases are becoming increasingly important: from approximately 10 percent three years ago to an expected figure of 20 percent three years from now.

Box 4.4 *(Source: McKinsey&Company)*

PORTFOLIO BREAKDOWN OVER PRODUCT CATEGORIES, %

	3 yrs ago	**last year**	**3 yrs from now**
Operational lease	11%	14%	19%
Financial lease	89%	86%	81%

100% = 118 companies

Many leasing companies expect that third-party distributors such as manufacturers and, especially, bank branches, will take on an increasing role as distribution channels for new business in the years to come. Leasing companies also expected that both independent distributors and direct sales to end customers / clients would lose market share.

Box 4.5 *(Source: McKinsey&Company)*

DIVISION OF NEW PRODUCTION OVER DISTRIBUTION CHANNELS, %

	3 yrs ago	**last year**	**3 yrs from now**
Manufacturers	14,1%	14,6%	15,6%
Bank branches	21,0%	28,8%	31,9%
Independent distributors	19,4%	17,2%	15,0%
Direct sales to end customers / clients	45,5%	39,4%	37,5%

100% = 105 companies

Leasing companies expect the market to grow. Only 12 percent of our research population thought that the leasing market would shrink or remain constant in the coming years. The majority believed that the market would grow by 1 to 5 percent per year (30 percent of respondents) or 6 to 10 percent per year (33 percent). A quarter of the respondents expected the leasing market to grow by 10 percent or more per year. Leasing companies are less optimistic about the future profitability of the market. Most marketing executives thought that profitability would shrink (43 percent) or remain the same (29 percent). Only 28 percent of the marketing executives were quite optimistic about profit trends.

Box 4.6 *(Source: McKinsey&Company)*

OPINIONS ON CHANGES IN THE LEASE MARKET IN THE NEXT THREE YEARS, %

SIZE WILL .....

Grow by 10% or more per year:	25%
Grow by 5-10% per year:	33%
Grow somewhat by 1-5% per year:	30%
Remain the same:	9%
Shrink a little by 1-5% per year:	3%

PROFITABILITY WILL .....

Grow considerably:	2%
Grow:	10%
Grow somewhat:	16%
Remain the same:	29%
Shrink a little:	35%
Shrink:	8%

100% = 115 companies

Most leasing companies (41 percent) expect a (major or minor) shift from purchasing towards leasing in their main line of business. 27 percent of the executives expected no change. Only 16 percent thought there will be a small change in the direction of purchasing. A further 16 percent had no clear expectations on this point.

Box 4.7 *(Source: McKinsey&Company)*

EXPECTATIONS FOR PURCHASE-TO-LEASING RATIO IN MAIN LINE OF BUSINESS, %

Small change in direction of purchase:	16%
No change:	27%
Small change in direction of leasing:	37%
Large change in direction of leasing:	4%
Do not know:	16%

100% = 118 companies

Fiscal advantages will soon no longer be the most important added value of lease products. Flexibility and cost or funding advantages will become more important sources of added value to lessees. According to the respondents, even advantages like liquidity and convenience were likely to become more important than fiscal benefits. Buying factors such as "limiting residual value risk" and "outsourcing of non-core activities" would not gain in importance.

Box 4.8 *(Source: McKinsey&Company)*

IMPORTANCE FOR VALUE ADDED OF LEASING TO END USER/LESSEE

-	Fiscal advantages
+/-	Limiting residual value risk
+/-	Outsourcing of non-core activities
+	Flexibility
+	Cost/funding advantages
+	Liquidity
+	Convenience

With regard to the expected value proposition in the next three years, almost half the companies expected they would have to offer more customer benefits for roughly the same price. A quarter of the respondents expected roughly the same customer benefits for a lower or the same price. Only 1 percent hoped to be able to offer fewer customer benefits for a lower price.

Box 4.9 *(Source: McKinsey&Company)*

EXPECTATION OF VALUE PROPOSITION IN THE NEXT THREE YEARS, %

Roughly the same customer benefits for roughly the same price:	10%
More customer benefits for roughly the same price:	49%
Roughly the same customer benefits for a lower price:	15%
Fewer customer benefits for a lower price:	1%
More customer benefits for a higher price:	25%

100% = 107 companies

To sum up: leasing companies expect to have to pedal harder for the same reward in future. This emphasizes the need to rethink and revamp marketing strategies. The opportunity for European leasing companies is significant, but the effort is equally monumental.

The leasing companies best able to meet the marketing challenges of today and tomorrow will be those that manage the following four strategic challenges effectively: creating a customer focus, updating the product development program, pricing leasing products competitively and putting a productive information architecture in place.

4.5. MARKETING CHALLENGES

Managing all the above marketing challenges properly will be the ticket required for admission to the new competitive game. In the remainder of this chapter, we will discuss these challenges in relation to some of the results of our survey.

4.5.1 CREATING A CUSTOMER FOCUS

Identifying and fulfilling customer needs and managing customers more comprehensively are increasingly important activities for marketing in the leasing industry. According to the survey, almost three quarters of marketing executives thought that marketing was not or would not be "just" a support discipline for sales or "merely" the promotion of lease products and services to customers.

Box 4.10 *(Source: McKinsey&Company)*

DESCRIPTION ROLE OF MARKETING, %

	3 yrs ago	**last year**	**3 yrs from now**
Marketing is a support discipline for sales	55%	31%	18%
Marketing is the promotion of our products to customers	18%	28%	9%
Marketing is the identification and fulfillment of customer needs	27%	41%	73%

Managing the customer was and would remain the most important marketing activity of a leasing company. This is in line with other results of our survey, for instance:

1. Customer satisfaction is the topic most frequently researched on a regular basis amongst leasing companies. Sixty-three percent of the marketing executives agreed that this research was of the utmost importance, more so, for example, than regular research on demand estimates (34 percent), prices and pricing (23 percent) or promotion effectiveness (17 percent).

Box 4.11 *(Source: McKinsey&Company)*

MARKET RESEARCH TOPICS EMPLOYED ON A REGULAR BASIS, %	
Customer satisfaction:	63%
Corporate image and positioning:	44%
Market segmentation:	40%
New product development:	36%
Demand estimates:	34%
Prices and pricing:	23%
Promotion effectiveness:	17%
Other:	9%

2. Building long-term relationships with customers is replacing the traditional attitude of selling to anyone who wants to buy and differentiating market segments on the basis of the products and services offered.

Box 4.12 *(Source: McKinsey&Company)*

ORIENTATION OF THE COMPANY, %

	3 yrs ago	**last year**	**3 yrs from now**
Selling to anyone who wants to buy our products	44%	11%	7%
Focusing on advertisements/ promotion to generate leads	6%	4%	5%
Differentiating products for different market segments	21%	39%	24%
Building long-term relationships with customers	29%	46%	64%

There are two main ways of achieving excellence in the customer focus of a leasing company: improving the quality of the sales force and forming partnerships with customers.

Sales force quality can be improved in at least three ways:

1. *Train the staff.* Most leasing companies recognize the importance of training sales people in marketing skills, theories and methods. Seventy-two percent of the research population thought that training sales and marketing staff was important (28 percent) or very important (44 percent). Training all other employees in marketing skills, theories and approaches was considered important too. Most leasing companies realize that marketing skills and approaches have to be understood widely, not just in the marketing and sales department, if the entire organization is to be customer-driven.

Box 4.13 *(Source: McKinsey&Company)*

OPINION IMPORTANCE OF TRAINING PERSONNEL, %

MARKETING PERSONNEL	
Very important:	44%
Important:	26%
Somewhat important:	12%
Not so important:	4%
No opinion:	14%
OTHER PERSONNEL	
Very important:	19%
Important:	40%
Somewhat important:	19%
Not so important:	16%
No opinion:	6%

100% = 118 Companies

2. *Enlarge the variable component of compensation.* Variable compensation is an important tool for creating or building a customer orientation. A salesman whose income depends to a large degree on his performance is eager to identify and fulfill not only the explicit but also the implicit needs of the customer. Although many leasing companies give their sales forces little or no variable compensation, marketing executives felt that the variable component would increase over time. Three years ago, only 14 percent of leasing company sales forces had a variable income component of more than 20 percent of their total income. Three years from now, the number will be around twice as high.

Box 4.14 *(Source: McKinsey&Company)*

VARIABLE COMPONENT OF REMUNERATION FOR SALES PERSONNEL, %

Percent of total pay	3 yrs ago	last year	3 yrs from now
> 20%	14%	20%	27%
1-20%	35%	36%	36%
0%	51%	44%	37%

100% = 99 Companies

3. *Spend more time with your customers.* Excellent companies know what goes on in their customers' markets because they listen carefully. Three years ago, 47 percent of the respondents' sales forces spent only about 40 percent of their total working time at the customer. Three years from now, this figure will be around 75 percent.

Box 4.15 *(Source: McKinsey&Company)*

TIME SALES PERSONNEL SPEND WITH CUSTOMERS, PERCENTAGE OF COMPANIES

Percent of total working time	3 yrs ago	last year	3 yrs from now
>40%	47%	58%	76%
<40%	53%	42%	24%

100% = 102 Companies

The need to form customer partnerships, our second approach to creating a customer focus, has been recognized by most leasing companies. Very few have actually done it, however.

Establishing true customer partnerships can be a sustainable and very powerful supplementary strategy to achieve superior customer satisfaction, especially in the more mature areas of the leasing industry where they offer an attractive alternative to cut-throat, price-based competition. Customer partnerships are based on the idea that both companies, customer and supplier, can build core capabilities and use these to achieve superior customer satisfaction. Customer partnerships can add value (1) because each partner can concentrate on its own skills and capabilities. A shipping company, for example, may prefer to concentrate on finding the best logistical solution for its customers, i.e., the "software", while outsourcing the residual risks of the "hardware" to its leasing partners, (2) by cross-fertilization of ideas between the parties, which also helps to reinforce the relationship and (3) by lowering costs in the business system of both the seller and the buyer.

To create productive customer partnerships, leasing companies need to develop a unique capability-based win-win partnership proposition, as many industrial companies have done over the last few years.

4.5.2 UPDATING THE PRODUCT DEVELOPMENT PROGRAM

The development and marketing of new products has been referred to as the "life blood" of any company. Historically, new product development (NPD) was always an adjunct to the mainstream of marketing management. Today, with the increasingly narrow premium that can be extracted from "me too" products, NPD is becoming a critical marketing process in its own right. In the leasing industry, NPD is an attractive alternative to price-based competition. It is one of the most powerful strategies for increasing the profit margin. However, few leasing companies have outstanding track records in NPD.

To be an outstanding innovator, a company has to manage four overlapping elements of effective NPD:

1. Set NPD goals and objectives. The leasing company should be clear about:

- The nature of the NPD challenge. The focus of the effort obviously depends on the combination of the skills of the leasing company and the assessment of high-opportunity segments.
- How time-critical NPD is. The timing of product launch is crucial: new leasing products not only have to be new to the company, but to the leasing industry as well.
- The scale of the expected benefits. The amount of benefit that can be expected from NPD should be established from the start. An NPD strategy should be realistic in terms of the expected bottom line impact, yet ambitious enough to stimulate radical thinking.

2. Second, the NPD portfolio has to be balanced by understanding the different types of NPD which will be appropriate to different market segments and the technologies and skills which will be needed to realize them. Don't overstretch; box out early where you can get the "biggest bang for the buck".

3. The appropriate level of resources to be invested in NPD has to be evaluated against a realistic estimate of returns.

4. Finally, the NPD organization has to be managed. If a leasing company wants to improve its NPD effectiveness in the long term, not even a clear NPD strategy, a balanced NPD portfolio and sufficient investment will be enough on their own. Long-term innovativeness requires a shift in values and attitudes to NPD throughout the entire company.

Leasing companies should consider:

- Using "aspiration-based strategies". Successful innovators in industry find ways of marrying dream-driven aspirations with industry practicalities by defining an innovation strategy with guidelines that will not hamper creativity, but rather help focus innovation "bets" on high potential opportunities.

- Creating a "heaven for innovators", i.e., an environment that fosters innovation. This is the way to attract, motivate and retain the type of people who will generate future growth.

NPD is a key determinant of competitive success. Constantly seeking to improve existing products and / or coming up with new ones is one of the characteristics of successful companies.

4.5.3 PRICING LEASING PRODUCTS COMPETITIVELY

Pricing can be the business lever with the greatest bottom-line impact. It drives the amount of money the company makes by balancing the costs of supplying the product against the benefits provided to the customer. Leasing companies are aware of this. Our survey shows that the availability of information on all aspects of pricing is increasing. High-level pricing skills are, and will continue to be, more important than ever before, according to respondents. Most leasing companies agree that pricing information is still improving, which, together with a more mature market, has contributed to the cut-throat, price-based competition we now see in most segments of the leasing market.

Most leasing companies can no longer maintain profits simply by raising prices. The key question therefore becomes: what is the best way to manage this crucial marketing lever? Excellence in business marketing is about capturing the real economic surplus by gaining a better understanding of the customers' perception of value.

Leasing companies should move from cost- or competitor-based pricing to value-based pricing, avoiding underpricing or the launch of products that customers regard as over-expensive. The three major "pricing-to-value" questions are as follows:

1. *What product attributes do customers value?* The aim here is to understand how customers value product/price combinations, and what they value about products in particular. This entails gaining a complete understanding of customers' views, not only regarding "hard" benefits (e.g., fiscal advantages, lower residual value risks, flexibility, and funding advantages) but also "soft" benefits (such as the image of the leasing company).

2. *What competing products do customer segments consider as alternatives to leasing products?* The aim is to identify customer groups for which similar product attributes and price levels in a range of products/services provide similar (real or perceived) value. Price itself can play a significant role in shaping perceptions and an awareness of some of the behavioral aspects of pricing may be useful, for instance how 'reference pricing' is being used to establish value. Customers evaluate actual prices in relation to reference prices, which are prices they consider fair. Reference prices can be influenced: for example, American Express and Chemical Bank use promotion and advertising strategies for this purpose.

3. *What price optimizes the combination of perceived value and profits?* The first step here is to determine how demand for a lease product will vary as a function of its price, and the price then has to be set at the level which optimizes profit. An understanding of "transaction pricing" will ensure that the product/service is not being "given away" and that, in each case, as much as possible of the total value available to the buyer and seller remains with the seller. The key is how to decide the exact price to assign to each customer transaction, and how to structure that transaction.

Failure to understand the value that customers perceive in a leasing product will, at best, mean that pricing opportunities are missed and, at worst, can result in competitive pricing behavior, which can lead to a spiral of decline and most undesirable price wars.

The losses from price wars almost invariably outweigh any gains (that is, the increase in volume required to compensate for lost profit is unlikely to be achieved), and the much-cited rationale that price wars drive poor performers out of the market is rarely true. This is because (1) price advantages are often short-lived (particularly in commodity financial products), (2) the capacity rarely goes away, and (3) industry shake-outs seldom occur in the European financial services industry.

The biggest problem of all is that price competition in general, and price wars in particular, increase customers' price sensitivity, and therefore do lasting damage to price perceptions - i.e., what constitutes a fair price according to customers. However, there are many ways to avoid price wars. Companies facing a (potential) price-based competitive attack can respond (proactively) by: (1) performing non-price activities (never shift the competitive playing field from benefits to price), (2) exploiting niches (customer, product or channel niches),

(3) "hiding from the war" or (4) seeking long-term contracts and partnerships with key customers.

4.5.4 PUTTING A PRODUCTIVE INFORMATION ARCHITECTURE IN PLACE

Information in general and marketing information in particular is a key asset for leasing companies, and is becoming a more important avenue to exploit as sources proliferate and technology advances. However, it is also becoming harder to manage.

Judging by the annual market research budget reported by respondents, most leasing companies are aware of the strategic importance of information: the average annual budget for market research three years from now is expected to be three times as high as it was three years ago.

Box 4.16 *(Source: McKinsey&Company)*

BUDGET FOR MARKET RESEARCH, INDEX, LAST YEAR = 100

3 yrs ago	**last year**	**3 yrs from now**
43	100	135

Internal and competitor information will become available in ever greater amounts. But most leasing companies also expect that the quantity of information on customer needs and integrated customer data bases will make a quantum leap in the next three years.

Box 4.17 *(Source: McKinsey&Company)*

AVAILABILITY OF MARKETING INFORMATION ON AN ON-GOING BASIS, PERCENT OF COMPANIES AVAILABLE

	3 yrs ago	**last year**	**3 yrs from now**
Internal information (prices, promotion, spending, profitability)	76%	88%	93%
External information on competitors	58%	75%	82%
Detailed information on customer needs	30%	43%	69%
Integrated customer databases	30%	50%	82%

Two years from now, approximately 60 percent of respondents will be using database marketing, compared to 37 percent today.

Box 4.18 *(Source: McKinsey&Company)*

USE OF DATABASE MARKETING, %

Right now:	yes = 37%; no = 63%
Within two years:	yes = 60%; no = 38%; do not know = 2%

100% = 115 Companies

Yet at the same time, respondents say that market research is the least important activity of the marketing function. This seems to contradict the above points somewhat: it seems that leasing companies are not yet ready to put their money where their mouth is. Most leasing companies are still paying little attention to improving the use of information and the methods and techniques of data gathering.

Box 4.19 *(Source: McKinsey&Company)*

RELATIVELY OF IMPORTANCE IN MARKETING FUNCTION, AVERAGE ON SCALE	
Customer satisfaction	4,5
Product development	4,3
Sales	4,2
Pricing	4,1
Competitor analysis	3,8
Distribution strategy	3,7
Market research	3,3

1 = unimportant; 2 = relatively unimportant; 3 = neither unimportant nor important; 4 = relatively important; 5 = very important

In general, the increased variety and complexity of information enables leasing companies to radically improve the quality of marketing decisions, provided the risk of information overload can be avoided. Advanced technology allows for more frequent monitoring, finer geographic and demographic cuts and an increased number of relevant and available measures.

However, the marketing function often fails to appreciate the full potential of this kind of technology: in many cases, a history of poor data has led to a culture which is not rigorously fact-based, even though management increasingly recognizes the need for a strictly fact-based attitude. The potential benefits of improved information management combined with an improved technological infrastructure are enormous.

Improved information management leads to: (1) a better understanding of the key success factors of the leasing market and an improved understanding of the difference between what actually happened versus what could have happened in the market. This can help overcome problems of "not being able to see the wood for the trees", (2) more and better knowledge of the customer and (3) faster analyses in order to spend more time considering and exploring a particular issue.

The opportunity to design information flows that can support the marketing decision process could therefore be critical for achieving competitive advantage in the future. Learning from marketing information involves identifying patterns and relationships in order to anticipate customer needs and competitive actions and reactions. Accordingly, designing and managing information flows is probably the most powerful management task.

To build a more productive information architecture, leasing companies must activate their "sensors", i.e. their sales forces, in order to obtain reliable and valid data. The quality of the information used to support marketing and management decisions depends to a large extent on this interface between the leasing company and its environment. Leasing companies have to be aware that high quality (marketing) information and information systems will play a critical role in making the changes needed to achieve marketing excellence.

Chase Manhattan, an American best practice example, gives the following explicit advice for facilitating IT development and use:

- *Define marketing information needs before defining information systems.* In other words: determine information requirements carefully and review them regularly.

- *Try it, then fix it.* Only by testing and using results can the needs ultimately be defined.

- *Leverage externally available competence.* Numerous software products have been developed to help turn marketing data into usable information.

- *Understand trade-offs.* Consciously weigh cost against value and timeliness against accuracy in specifying information requirements.

- *React to the changing environment.* Regularly challenge conventional assumptions about the business and be prepared to alter information requirements as business conditions change.

4.6 CONCLUSION

To meet the demands of the new and more complex environment, leasing companies will have to make the transition from the second to the third or preferably the fourth era of marketing. They have to use the old tools - the traditional 4 Ps of the marketing mix - in a new way and start to use the new ones. They will have to rethink their objectives, redevelop marketing strategies, redesign the process of marketing and recreate their marketing approach. This represents a profound change that must be driven by CEOs as well as their marketing executives.

Chapter 5 Partnership management

5.1 INTRODUCTION

All marketers face the challenge of understanding and influencing the customer's buying decisions. However, the business-to-business marketer's ability to do this effectively is complicated by varying but fundamental problems:

- Specific buying decisions can be inherently complicated processes, often involving several decision-makers with different needs. Understanding and influencing customer buying decisions are core skills for the marketer attempting to optimize the composition and behaviors of a customer portfolio.
- The purchase process is seldom uniform across a customer base for any one product, compounding the challenges of developing effective marketing programs.
- In the case of large and complex account relationships, there is often a need to understand and influence a large number of separate decisions in an integrated manner.
- Constant changes in organizations, decision processes, decision participants, and customer needs often change the rules of the game and require the marketer to adapt continuously.

'Partnership management' is the most effective tool for handling these major challenges, and has been a frequently debated topic for many years. It has moved in and out of favor as organizations have struggled with different ways of handling their corporate client bases. Partnership management is now once more a hot topic in many institutions, yet relatively few have a sharp understanding of the ingredients for success.

Box 5.1 *(Source: McKinsey&Company)*

LEASING AND PARTNERSHIP MANAGEMENT: A SUB-OPTIMAL RELATIONSHIP

Leasing is a difficult arena in which partnership management has often been ineffective. There is opportunity to refine partnership management approaches by a systematic redesign process which tailors models to varied needs across the spectrum of corporate leasing clients.

- Leasing companies are facing increased pressure on their corporate business economics and need to leverage partnerships into higher value added products, maximizing overall account officer productivity.

- Traditional partnership management approaches have typically been undifferentiated and founded on increasingly inappropriate skill sets and internal processes which have failed to capture the potential benefits of deeper client penetration and improved service quality.

- Many leasing companies now need to reappraise their approach to partnership management through a systematic review of client segmentation, partnership management roles and organization management processes, underpinned by a commitment to sustained implementation.

The purpose of this chapter is to back up a theoretical discussion of important issues with the practical implications. It gives greater depth to the main message of Chapter four: be aware of the vital importance - in terms of added value - of proactively managing the relationships between a leasing company and its external environment in general, and its customers in particular.

The specific aims of this chapter are as follows:

- It places partnership management in the context of the financial industry and provides different frameworks for thinking through marketing improvements in leasing companies.
- It explores examples of 'best practice' approaches, and shows how effective partnership management can really be.
- It discusses the critical elements of putting partnership management into practice.

5.2 DEFINITION OF PARTNERSHIP MANAGEMENT

Ever cheaper and more powerful IT and targeted media are allowing marketers to seek new answers to old questions, such as: are my customers sufficiently different to justify tailored offerings; can I deliver these offerings profitably; is my current organization able to deliver them to the customer; if not, how should I reorganize?

Contrary to popular belief, the answers do not lie in specialized technical areas like IT, neural networks and multimedia. These are classic strategic questions that all marketers have always asked. In a sense, all of them are about partnership management.

Box 5.2 *(Source: McKinsey&Company)*

PARTNERSHIPS

Partnerships are important enough to be a new "P" for industrial/-commercial marketers:

- Business-to-business companies are increasingly turning to partnerships as a powerful tool for sales and profit growth, competitive advantage, and customer loyalty.

- There are growing numbers of companies who have achieved demonstrated impact.

- Other Ps are often tapped out or provide limited degrees of freedom; partnerships offer largely untapped potential with often many degrees of freedom.

The ideal situation can be described as follows: when we have a good ongoing relationship, we can use what we know to capture and retain a large share of customer value without appearing intrusive. Partnership Management takes many names and forms: Continuous Predictive Marketing (CPM), Continuous Responsive Marketing (CRM) or World Class Database Marketing (WCDM). Every definition involves creating value through iterative attempts to deliver individually tailored and integrated solutions to customer problems.

Partnership management is a marketing approach that seeks to build close relationships between a company and its (most attractive) customers in order to encourage them to concentrate a disproportionately large proportion of their value with that company. In other words, business-to-business partnerships are the joining together of two or more companies for the purpose of improving customer value (either by strengthening a value proposition or improving its execution), accomplished by means of the partial integration of selected business system elements and joint actions by the partners. In a sense, a partnership is an intermediate option between a merger and a contract, a long-term trust-based relationship providing unique benefits to both parties, thus enhancing the industry profit and the partners' competitiveness. A 'win-win' situation is therefore a prerequisite.

Effective partnership management develops its target programs and timing using a hypothesis-driven approach combined with substantial fact-based analysis. It uses, but is never driven by, data analysis techniques such as regression or neural networks. Partnership management entails developing and continuously updating the company's knowledge of existing and forecasts of future needs for each customer, and tailoring the value proposition as closely to those needs as makes economic sense.

Box 5.3 *(Source: McKinsey&Company)*

KEY ATTRIBUTES OF PARTNERSHIP MANAGEMENT

- Build overall company value by managing the potential of individual customers (e.g., tailor value propositions to customers; have a clear understanding of the attractiveness of customers to a company).

- Use information and technology to identify and deliver more finely tailored value propositions.

- Gain a broader and deeper understanding of what works and what does not (e.g., use multiple targeted initiatives against individual customers; test, track, and evaluate at both customer and program level; use multiple channels).

Perhaps the concept of partnership management is best understood by reviewing the resulting changes in an organization's marketing mindset and the supporting organizational requirements (see box 5.4).

Box 5.4 *(Source: McKinsey&Company)*

CHARACTERISTICS OF MASS MARKETING AND PARTNERSHIP MANAGEMENT

BEST PRACTICE MASS MARKETING

Buyers / product managers selling one product at a time to as many customers as possible

Any customer is a good customer

Passive customers

Counting advertising impressions

Bombarding the market

Single-channel distribution

"We have the data we need"

Current needs

PARTNERSHIP MANAGEMENT

Customer managers selling as many products as possible to one customer at the time

Some customers are much more valuable than others

Involved participants

Measuring advertising responses

Building relationships

Multi-channel distribution

"We use the data we have and try to capture more"

Latent needs as well

Partnerships deliver bottom-line value and strategic advantage, especially in service industries being commoditized by price competition. Although price competition has proved ineffective as a means to increase share in most service industries, competitors continue to battle on price - commoditizing the industry and leading to poor returns and sub-optimum product/service offerings. Partnerships neutralize the market share implications of pricing by improving the product/service offering and refocusing customer attention away from price.

Partnership management often leads to breakthrough results: improved customer value based on product/service offerings, an antagonistic relationship replaced by a partner-like relationship and a competitive moat regenerated by continual upgrading of the partnership (box 5.5).

Box 5.5 *(Source: McKinsey&Company)*

A NEW PARADIGM

PARTNERSHIP ELEMENT

- *Commitment to solve business problems together.* <u>Value to customer</u>: improved product/service offering, supplier perceived as business partner, multiple contact points established.

- *Price and terms flexibility to meet short-term customer requirements.* <u>Value to customer</u>: ability to manage cash-flow or defer tax (if legally acceptable).

- *Partner to smooth future price movements.* <u>Value to customer</u>: predictable price (better investment planning, better tax planning), reduced ongoing negotiation effort, guaranteed price fairness (customer contact focused on constructive discussion).

Several leading financial companies are delivering strong financial performances by applying partnership management precepts. Some companies - such as Goldman Sachs, Morgan Stanley and Merrill Lynch - collect and use extensive amounts of information about individual customers as a basis for targeted actions that increase realizable customer value at all stages of the relationship. Other leading edge marketers use partnership management techniques to boost both revenue growth and returns.

5.3 DIMENSIONS OF PARTNERSHIP MANAGEMENT

Partnership management involves moving away from traditional mass marketing towards more targeted, more timely and deeper relationships.

Each of the three underlying dimensions of who?, what? and when? should be examined to gain a good understanding of best practice in the area.

5.3.1 WHO?

Partnership management is based on an orientation to customer profitability rather than product profitability. Its data-driven approach bases marketing actions on their tested and proven ability to increase revenues and / or reduce costs.

This view also involves focusing on those customers with the greatest value-building opportunities; often the economic cost of tailoring partnership management activities is most lucrative with the top 20 percent of the market. This view of value potential combines both overall category value and a company's ability to capture that value.

5.3.2 WHAT?

Partnership management identifies customer relationship stages and marketing levers which facilitate differentiated communication with customers (see also paragraph 5.6). By putting this knowledge to use, leasing companies can stimulate sales to target customer categories, capture a disproportionate share of the value of these customers, and do so very profitably.

5.3.3 WHEN?

'When' to act can mean being responsive, predictive, or both, as circumstances dictate. The partnership management view of the importance of time and timing can substantially redefine marketing activities, in terms of both identifying attractive businesses and suggesting the value of targeted retention activities.

5.4 BENEFITS OF PARTNERSHIP MANAGEMENT

Organizations frequently have difficulty assessing the potential value of partnership management. However, a number of analyses and insights can be used to help demonstrate the benefits of partnership management strategies:

- *Understand the customer base.* Many companies have a limited understanding of the profitability of different customer segments, the depth of their relationship with each customer, and the importance of specific customer segments to their firm's overall financial performance. Developing this understanding further frequently provides significant new insights and often creates a strong incentive to launch a partnership management effort.

- *Benchmark best practice.* To assess the potential benefits of a partnership management strategy, leasing organizations can quantify the gap between a company's performance and industry best practice along the critical dimensions for a partnership management strategy. The most significant challenge in these analyses is to identify the relevant benchmarking dimensions.

- *Conduct market research.* While benchmarking against national or international averages helps identify the potential partnership management opportunities, some organizations have found that quick market research analyses provide compelling insights into specific local benchmarks and competitors.

5.4.1 UNDERSTAND THE CUSTOMER BASE

To develop a full understanding of their existing customer base, leasing companies have to address a wide range of issues concerning the profitability and depth of relationships with different customer segments. Analysis of these issues can also help to illuminate the partnership management levers that may help to create the most significant value (box 5.6).

Box 5.6 *(Source: McKinsey&Company)*

KEY ISSUES TO ADDRESS TO UNDERSTAND CUSTOMER BASE

- *What percentage of sales and profits is accounted for by different segments of customers?* What are the demographic and behavioral characteristics of the company's most attractive customers? What percentage of customers have the attributes?

- *What is the depth of relationship with different segments of customers?* How many accounts on average do different segments of customers have? What is the average balance on these accounts?

- *What happens to different groups of customers over time?* How many customers (by segment) leave each year? What is the cost of acquiring different groups of customers?

A first step towards understanding the customer base is assessing the profitability of different groups of customers. For most companies, a relatively small percentage of customers account for a disproportionately large share of profits. This is, for example, true of most financial institutions. Among the retail customers at Banc One, a small fraction of the retail customers account for over 100 percent of the profits, with the remaining customers actually, on average, losing money for the bank.

At another financial institution, 17 percent of customers contributed 89 percent of profits. Such customer profitability analyses focus companies on the importance of different customer groups - a key first step in understanding the potential benefits of a partnership management strategy.

In addition, organizations frequently have a limited understanding of the depth of the relationships they have with each customer or the potential impact of increasing them. For example, a financial institution may have strong relationships with a few customers, but a relatively limited "share of wallet" for many others.

This varying depth of relationship contributes to different levels of profitability for each segment, but also helps to demonstrate the potential benefits of developing a partnership management strategy to increase the number of relationships per customer. If, for example, the depth of relationship could be increased in specific customer segments, the firm could generate significant incremental value.

These varying customer profitability levels demonstrate the importance of retaining the particularly attractive customer segments. However, additional analyses frequently demonstrate that companies have poor retention. At one retailer, 50 percent of the store's best customers churned annually while a financial institution found that many of its mortgage customers refinanced before the mortgage was profitable. These facts demonstrate the importance of improving retention. Partnership management strategies can be developed to focus on the value created through retention. The various analyses of the customer base and the impact of different partnership management levers can be combined to demonstrate the potential impact of an overall partnership management strategy.

5.4.2 BENCHMARK BEST PRACTICES

Another way to estimate the value of a partnership management strategy is to benchmark a company's performance against industry best practices along critical partnership management dimensions. The primary challenge in these situations is to identify the relevant dimensions (box 5.7). These benchmark analyses help to illustrate, for example, the cross-selling opportunities that exist.

Box 5.7 *(Source: McKinsey&Company)*

ILLUSTRATIVE PARTNERSHIP MANAGEMENT MEASURES FOR BENCHMARKING PERFORMANCE

BANKING

Accounts/households

Balances/account

"Share of wallet"

Average length of customer relationship

Product specific benchmarks (e.g., for credit cards, home equity loans)

RETAILING

Frequency of purchase

Visits/year

Average purchase size

Annual sales of department store type

CREDIT CARD

Receivables/account

% revolvers

Retention

% accounts active

Charge-off as % of receivables

5.4.3 CONDUCT MARKET RESEARCH

Conducting some quick market research can provide organizations with valuable information about the performance of their leading competitors. Market research can offer the following benefits: it identifies the performance of leading competitors along relevant dimensions, it provides local/product-specific benchmarks for analysis (rather than [national] averages), it provides insights into the drivers of customer behavior and it can be accomplished in a few weeks. Market research can be conducted in a three-phase process (see box 5.8).

Box 5.8 *(Source: McKinsey&Company)*

STEPS REQUIRED FOR QUICK MARKET RESEARCH, BANK EXAMPLE

ORGANIZE FOCUS GROUPS

Identify issues that were important to small business bank customers, especially with regard to the identified core processes. Prioritize these issues in terms of their importance to the customer. Provide input to the customer survey to be designed later. Format: in each market, two groups of 8-10 people were interviewed, one of customers, one non-customers. Logistics and moderator were outsourced.

CONDUCT PHONE SURVEY

Provide a database for an understanding of the market position and an actionable basis for customer segmentation. Format: 60 multiple-response questions were asked, conduction of the survey was outsourced.

ASSESS OPPORTUNITY

Estimate value creation potential of moving client to competitors' levels of performance for both cross-selling and customer acquisition.

Market research illustrates the gap between the organization's own performance and that of relevant local competitors.

5.5 CUSTOMER LIFETIME VALUE ANALYSIS AND PARTNERSHIP MANAGEMENT

Partnership management calls for an approach that will help organizations make strategic choices about where to invest their marketing resources. Customer lifetime value analysis (CLV) is the primary analytical tool for making such decisions.

Box 5.9 *(Source: McKinsey&Company)*

STRATEGIC CHOICES IN PARTNERSHIP MANAGEMENT ENGAGEMENTS

How much value is created through different partnership management levers?

- Acquiring new customers?
- Promoting/cross-selling existing customers?
- Increasing customer retention?

Companies developing partnership management strategies assess their overall franchise value in terms of the lifetime value of their customers. This framework is fundamentally different from the traditional view of assessing a company's value in terms of the individual product lines (box 5.10).

Box 5.10 *(Source: McKinsey&Company)*

ASSESS COMPANY VALUE IN TERMS OF LIFETIME VALUE TO CUSTOMERS

TRADITIONAL VIEW

Total value = value of product A + value of product B + value of product C

LIFETIME VALUE OF A CUSTOMER VIEW

Total value = value of a customer/segment (that is, value from product sales and retention over customer lifetime minus cost of acquisition/sales) * number of customers

Performing the basic calculations for CLV is relatively straightforward; simply discount the cash flows received from a customer over time. However, for a detailed CLV analysis other significant issues have to be addressed, such as the probability of product purchases, and estimated customer retention levels.

The value of these customer relationships varies widely across industries and among different customer segments within industries, and in all cases substantially exceeds the value of individual transactions. While CLV analysis provides insights into the value of customer relationships, it can also be useful in making resource allocation decisions about different acquisition channels.

To summarize, customer lifetime value in simple terms is the present value of the cash flows received from a particular customer over time, less the cost of acquiring the customer. The CLV concept helps leasing organizations to focus on the value they generate from specific customers, not from product groups.

5.6 DEVELOPING PARTNERSHIP MANAGEMENT STRATEGIES

CLV analysis raises a number of strategic issues about the potential value that can be created by applying each partnership management lever (box 5.11).

Box 5.11 *(Source: McKinsey&Company)*

STRATEGIC ISSUES RAISED BY CUSTOMER LIFETIME VALUE ANALYSIS

ACQUIRE

- Which channels are most attractive for acquisition?
- Which segments of customers should be acquired?
- How do acquisition costs vary by channel and customer group?
- What acquisition sources yield the most attractive customers?

PROMOTE/CROSS-SELL

- What products should be offered to each customer and/or segment?
- What is the return on investment of different promotional campaigns?
- What are the behavioral characteristics of the most attractive customers?
- What demographic information is correlated with the most attractive customers?

RETAIN

- What is the "effective lifetime" of an account?
- How do retention rates vary by customer and/or segment?
- What approaches to retaining attractive customers are most effective?

The objectives of a partnership management strategy can be grouped broadly into three categories:

- *Acquisition*. Identifying and attracting the highest value customers, while discouraging the acquisition of low value customers.
- *Promoting/cross-selling (usage stimulation)*. Increasing profitable usage (e.g., higher monthly spend on a credit card, higher monthly revolving balances on a credit card, higher balances in a current account, more frequent purchase of an item), cross-selling other related products or services (e.g., income protection insurance with loans, clothing made by same designer as a fragrance purchased) and encouraging economical usage.

- *Retention.* Increasing the likelihood of retention of high value customers, encouraging reactivation of high value customers whose usage has declined, and discouraging retention for marginal- to loss-making customers (e.g., introduce minimum balances and / or annual fees for current accounts and credit cards and force action on dormant accounts, i.e., reactivate or close them).

Acquisition

CLV analysis can help in defining the optimum customer acquisition channels and timing. For example, a leasing company may believe that customers who are acquired as students are particularly attractive, but find through CLV analysis that they are actually unlikely to ever have a positive net present value. CLV analysis may show that acquiring these customers upon graduation creates significantly more value.

Promotion/cross-selling

CLV analysis, combined with some form of segmentation, also provides insights into promotional or cross-selling opportunities. Demographic segmentation can shed light on the potential value of customers of different ages. However, behavioral segmentation typically provides the most compelling insights into the drivers of CLV. With an understanding of both demographic and behavioral characteristics, a leasing organization can begin to develop specific strategies that increase the value of these customer relationships.

Retention

Finally, CLV analysis provides information on the impact of discontinuing existing customers. In our credit card example, a partnership management strategy could increase the average retention and value of customer accounts. Several levers can be used to achieve any of the three broad partnership management goals:

- *Service.* Services which reflect customer preferences and economic value can be offered with the product in order to encourage purchase, profitable usage, and retention. American Airlines provides loyal travel customers with special services, including a separate reservations phone line, preferential seating, and class upgrades.

- *Pricing.* Pricing can be differentiated to address customers' price value trade-off, to encourage the loyalty of the most valuable customers and to channel usage into cost-effective behaviors for low-value segments. Providian (credit cards) uses customers' credit history and information about the other credit cards they hold to design optimum target offers for each prospective customer.

- *Cross-selling.* Products and services can be bundled or linked in a way that increases their attractiveness to high value customers. South African Bank offers tailored multi-product packages, including low-interest rate mortgages and pre-approved credit cards, to high value segments (e.g., doctors).

- *Event-based selling.* Offers can be made in response to specific trigger events. JC Penney Life (life insurance) uses special occasions like an upcoming 30th birthday to offer additional life insurance protection.

With creative combinations of program levers and goals, the opportunities for value creation are almost endless. Best-practice companies using partnership management often create a broad spectrum of strategies combining several levers and value-creation goals.

The degree of targeting in partnership management strategies can be categorized on three levels:

- *Mass.* Programs marketed toward all customers and in which participation is basically unrestricted. Objectives: creating and maintaining customer loyalty and obtaining maximum information at minimum cost.

- *Segment-based.* Programs offered to segments based on demographic profile or behavioral characteristics. Objectives: encouraging specific behavioral changes with bottom line impact while building a base of customer information.

- *Customer-tailored.* Programs with offers tailored to individuals, often communicated in a very personal way that is meaningful to the customer. Objective: building strong, high value, sustainable relationships.

As the degree of targeting increases, the opportunities and challenges also grow (box 5.12).

Box 5.12 *(Source: McKinsey&Company)*

OPPORTUNITIES AND CHALLENGES ACROSS STRATEGY TYPES

MASS-MARKET

Opportunities/benefits: can be introduced with minimal customer information and/or internal analytical skills; enables accumulation of information about customers/prospects to be used for future tailoring/targeting; permits customer self-selection into differentiated pricing or service based on behavior. Challenges/costs: easy to replicate; can be expensive to implement to broad audience; difficult to measure impact due to lack of control group; difficult to modify or terminate (becomes expected by customer).

SEGMENT-BASED

Opportunities/benefits: more efficient/effective marketing spend; lends well to measurement and improved tailoring/targeting using test and control groups; can be implemented on ad hoc basis within finite time frames and with no future obligation to customers. Challenges/costs: complexity in managing programs and customer segments; it requires good analytical skills for identifying customer segments and developing statistical models.

CUSTOMER-TAILORED

Opportunities/benefits: opportunity for most efficient/effective marketing spend (marketing to "segment of one"); difficult for competitors to replicate; potentially most powerful way to develop true relationships from the customer perspective; enables continuous learning about individual preferences and behavior; can be implemented on ad hoc basis within finite time frames and with no future obligation to customers. Challenges/costs: complexity in managing the overall customer relationship; it requires superior analytical and front-line skills as well as sophisticated IT systems in order to identify individual customer needs/preferences, ensure offers are initiated and followed through, and maximize learning to ensure continuous improvement in targeting.

Leasing companies may start at different levels of tailoring, depending on their customer knowledge and executional skills. The degree to which leasing companies should move toward customer-tailored strategies depends on several key factors. The most important of these is 'industry'.

The attractiveness of customer-tailored programs varies by industry depending on several factors. The value creation potential of customer-tailored strategies aimed at high product margins is relatively high in insurance firms.

In summary, CLV analysis provides unique insights into developing a partnership management strategy. Specifically, CLV analysis helps leasing organizations to understand the value created through customer acquisition, promotion, and retention.

5.7 DEVELOPING INFORMATION SYSTEMS TO DELIVER PARTNERSHIP MANAGEMENT

IT systems play a critical role in ensuring the high degree of integration required to implement continuous partnership management. We would like to share four key lessons we have learnt about building the information systems to support partnership management:

- Most partnership management efforts turn into misguided attempts to build all-seeing, all-knowing stocks of data.
- A value-driven approach to building IT capabilities for continuous partnership management can deliver value faster and set the stage for continuous learning.
- Off-the-shelf software and current hardware capabilities make it easier for new adopters to build capability than was the case for pioneers.

There are three main information systems requirements for effective partnership management:

- A marketing database: to consolidate key data from transaction systems, promotional campaigns and external sources.
- Analytical tools: to identify drivers of customer profitability and potential and translate into actionable customer segmentation schemes and predictive behavioral models.
- Links to operating systems: to coordinate multiple, integrated marketing communications and actions targeted at unique and often small customer and product segments.

The marketing database aggregates all the data required for effective partnership management. It provides fast, flexible access to data for different partnership management-related topics and supports the coding and processing of data for specific analyses, segmentation and proprietary modeling.

Analytical tools are required to "mine" the database. The purpose is to translate relationships between customers and transactions into transparent marketing-driven solutions. The result is increased efficiency of existing marketing and management activities. Furthermore, it creates a platform for increased management effectiveness, by generating insights into company-specific customer behavior which can become a basis for competitive advantage.

Partnership management requires links between database analytics and operations, in order to deliver the customer insights won. This provides a basis for managing much greater complexity and customization while preserving closed-loop discipline.

5.8 PARTNERSHIP MANAGEMENT APPROACHES

There are two distinct types of leasing companies working with large corporate customers - general leasing companies and focused leasing companies. Their partnership management needs and best practice approaches differ in important ways.

General

General leasing companies have broad product portfolios and typically aspire to serve corporate customers with a broad range of products. A general leasing company's approach to partnership management will be focused on a strong need to improve lending-based economics and to enhance the coordination of a broad product portfolio. Their priorities for partnership management are focused on the need to leverage traditionally strong relationships and enhance penetration across a wider product range.

With large corporates, a name-by-name segmentation strategy based on a leasing company's specific relationship with its customers is a critical first step. Segmentation may result in the identification of a number of client groupings, each of which is characterized by distinct product usage and decision-making behavior.

The partnership manager's business development role needs to be clearly separated off from other activities. Partnership managers' roles and skills should be aligned with those of corporate decision-makers. Some client segments are likely to warrant more than one partnership manager.

Performance measurement and evaluation should be driven by profit yardsticks, include peer review and capture actual behavior and activities. Partnerships plans are a key element of supporting processes and tools needed to shape a more teamwork-based general culture.

Focused

A focused leasing company's approach to partnership management will concentrate on the need to enhance coordination amongst highly competent product specialists, and to maintain a teamwork approach over long 'boom and bust' product cycles. Its customer segmentation will differ in important respects from that of a general leasing company; prospective fees and industry expertise are more useful criteria. The definition of roles will be driven by the highly specialized nature of its business, and will be closely tied to skills.

The measurement of economic performance is typically based around revenue and productivity yardsticks, while evaluation systems should reflect individual performance, team performance and contributions to building the franchise. Performance measurement and account management systems will include more qualitative criteria for individuals than for business units.

Best-practice approaches are always used to focus sales activities (segmentation should evolve from an undifferentiated to a needs-based approach, with "size of wallet" driving the intensity of the sales effort), leverage product specialists (increased segmentation will lead to better targeting of customers' product needs, promoting cross-selling and the identification of structured solutions), and improve sales force efficiency and effectiveness (a tailored, IT-based toolbox should be provided to enhance sales force efficiency and effectiveness).

Best practice approaches reflect the urgent need to develop a new and better value proposition more appropriate to the absolute potential of each customer. Successful implementation of partnership management requires a good fit between product capabilities and partnership management aspirations, a clear design for implementation, a well-executed pilot program, execution of a small number of key short-term tasks and a sustained focus on creating a partnership culture.

5.9 PARTNERSHIP MANAGEMENT STRATEGY DEVELOPMENT: AN EXAMPLE

Developing partnership management strategies generally includes six key steps based on defining value creation opportunities and ensuring learning through continuous testing.

Box 5.13 *(Source: McKinsey&Company)*

SIX KEY STEPS IN PROGRAM DEVELOPMENT

1. *Determine program objectives*: determine the overall goal of the partnership management program (acquisition, usage, retention); identify key levers and estimate the expected value of the program.

2. *Define target customers*: define target segments and / or individuals; determine available information to identify / profile these target customers.

3. *Brainstorm/screen program ideas*: identify potential program ideas; screen ideas based on e.g., likely customer perception, fit with other company goals / initiatives (for instance, image etc).

4. *Develop test programs*: define constraints (e.g., budget etc); determine details of test programs (offer specifics, communication vehicles, message / copy); finalize customer selection criteria for inclusion in the program.

5. *Define test and control groups*: confirm program variations to be tested (e.g., offer, communication vehicle, message, copy); set sample sizes; select variables to be measured and the appropriate time frame, e.g., response rate, customer profitability after three / twelve months.

6. *Conduct program and measure impact*: implement program; measure and track individual responses; analyze results; modify program design based on findings.

'Assurance' Bank (a disguised example) is a best case example of a company experienced in program development and the continuous test and learn process. The overall goal of this North American bank was to demonstrate the potential of partnership management and build baseline experience. Initial pilot tests were simple, occasion-based, cross-selling programs designed for immediate learning.

Broad client involvement ensured that a baseline experience was built. The program focused on moving key customer behavior levers. The programs lasted for one year, reflecting a readiness to build a long-term partnership management initiative. Significant skills were built in a select client group.

'Assurance' Bank learnt the following lessons concerning partnership management strategies:

- *Program design*. Revisit program objectives frequently throughout the program development process. Interesting ideas may unintentionally circumvent program objectives.
- *Test and control*. When conducting test and control groups, have clear value creation and learning objectives in mind, check that your test program elements drive these objectives and will facilitate future rollout.
- *Brainstorming*. Cross-functional teams provide a wider perspective. Also include front-line employees where possible: they know the customer best.
- *Customer team*. Ensure customer ownership and involvement at each step of the process. Without sufficient commitment and skill-building, momentum for testing and learning can quickly melt away.

5.10 KEY MESSAGES

Message 1. The strength of partnership management is derived from accepting long-term prices as exogenous, then shifting the focus to customer interactions from controllable dimensions of product and service offerings.

Message 2. Leasing companies can create value through partnership management strategies in an almost endless variety of ways by pursuing three typical partnership management goals (acquisition, usage stimulation, retention) with the use of a variety of levers (including product service, pricing and promotion).

Message 3. The degree of targeting in partnership management strategies can be categorized at three levels - mass, segment-specific, and customer-tailored - which offer increasing value to customers due to enhanced relationship-building capabilities, improved economics, and increased barriers to competitive reactions.

Message 4. Developing partnership management strategies requires a clear understanding of the value creation opportunity and a continuous test-and-learn approach. The approach to developing strategies with customers will vary depending on the leasing company's current customer information and key executional skills, as well as its commitment to partnership management as a fundamental value creation initiative.

Message 5. Communicating the vision, strategy and mechanisms of new partnership management approaches, not only throughout the leasing company but also to customers, is critical to success.

Message 6. Partnerships are an effective way of competing for share in a commoditizing industry like leasing. Price competition can be neutralized effectively. A deep understanding of the customer is a prerequisite. A far deeper understanding of the customer's business is required here than commoditizing industries typically have.

Message 7. The behavior of customers can be shaped by the effective use of a partnership.

These messages are important, because identifying the characteristics that make a relationship profitable and managing the portfolio so that more customers exhibit these characteristics is becoming the key driver of earnings growth in the leasing industry. Partnership management is the primary lever a leasing company holds to differentiate its service, maximize the profitability of each relationship, recognize needs and take an active role in proposing solutions and understanding customers' needs / usage of other non-traditional products.

To accomplish this, leasing companies must set a cultural change in motion that allows every level of the organization to support a true partnership management approach:

- Top management must embrace the idea and support it with a new set of incentives and career paths.
- Front-line account officers must change their criteria for success (compensation needs to be relationship-driven) and, as a result, the way they spend their time. Yardsticks need to be developed for tracking success in penetrating relationships, measuring customer satisfaction, and managing relationship-level profitability.
- Tools and yardsticks must be put in place to foster greater coordination between traditionally independent areas (product specialists and functional departments).

Building an effective cadre of partnership managers will require an evolution of the leasing company's understanding of and support for the role and value of partnership management. Partnership managers must have access to a wide array of information tools - such as information access tools (on-line systems), decision support systems (comparative pricing data) and productivity enhancement tools (financial forecasting applications, electronic messaging, document transfer, spreadsheets, and word processing) - if they are to serve all the needs of their customers and potential customers more productively.

Chapter 6 The future of leasing

6.1 INTRODUCTION

Now that leasing and the associated aspects of marketing have been dealt with in some detail, we would like to conclude with a chapter about how leasing is likely to develop in the future.

It is not an easy picture to paint. After all, leasing is not a self-contained product with a distinct, separate market. It is a product which is used in various branches of industry for different types of investment, like, for example, a bank loan. Exploring the future of leasing therefore means that developments in a large number of relevant sectors and countries have to be taken into account. An exhaustive study of these developments is obviously beyond the scope of this chapter, so we will limit ourselves to a few key areas.

The five most important factors influencing the future development of leasing can be summarized as follows:

1. The general economic development of a country and particularly developments in the volume of investment.
2. The nature of investments and the extent to which they are suitable for leasing.
3. Legislation on leasing.
4. The willingness of (potential) customers to use the lease product.
5. The product and marketing policy of suppliers in the leasing industry.

We will use these five factors as a guide in outlining the expected future developments.

6.2 GENERAL ECONOMIC DEVELOPMENTS

The size of the leasing market is primarily determined by general economic factors, and particularly by developments in the volume of investment. Leasing is a product that derives its existence from investment in capital goods. Economic growth is therefore a basic parameter for the size of its market.

Over the past few years, the leasing market in Europe has been showing clear signs of stagnation. In the eighties, we saw unparalleled growth. The size of the portfolio of all the leasing companies associated with Leaseurope increased from 21.5 billion ECU in 1984 to 95.2 billion ECU in 1990[8], representing an increase of 440% over 6 years. After 1990, however, there followed a few years of negative growth The volume of the Leaseurope companies' portfolio dropped back to 85.5 billion ECU in 1994. Since 1994, there have been some signs of recovery.

The less favorable development of the European leasing sector becomes strikingly clear when Europe is compared with other parts of the world. The following table shows that the trend in the European market is very different from developments in North America and Asia.[9]

Box 6.1 *(Source: World Leasing Yearbook (1995))*

LEASING: VOLUME AND GROWTH BY REGION 1992-1993

Region	*Annual volume*	*Growth in %*	*World market volume, %, '92*	*World market volume, %, '93*
N. America	132,5	+ 4,0	39,8	42,8
Asia	81,0	+ 0,2	25,3	26,1
Europe	79,9	- 19,7	31,0	25,8
S. America	9,3	+ 49,0	2,0	3,0
Australia	4,9	+4,0	1,3	1,6
Africa	2,0	+ 6,4	0,6	0,7
Total	**309,6**			

8 Leaseurope Annual report 1994

9 World Leasing Yearbook 1995, Euromoney Publications, Essex UK.

From these figures, it can be seen that the share of European leasing in the world market is decreasing. In one year, the European market share decreased from 31% to 25.8%. There are both economic and structural causes for this development.

The economic recession in Europe at the beginning of the nineties hit the leasing sector hard. The decrease in volume in Western European countries during that period was largely caused by a decrease in the volume of investment in capital goods. From a statistical point of view, the latter parameter proved to be the most import economic indicator for leasing. In countries where investment in capital goods slows down, leasing volume also declines. In the same way, a growth in leasing volume is also directly related to an increase in investment in capital goods.[10] The future of leasing thus largely depends on developments in the market for capital goods.

In addition to economic cyclicality, structural factors also play a role. From an international perspective, the economy of Western Europe is in a relatively weak competitive position, suggesting mediocre growth figures for the coming years. This also means modest growth expectations for leasing. The forecasts are worst for industrial companies. Western European industry is losing more and more ground to the emerging industrial countries in Asia, South America, and (in the near future) Eastern Europe. Western Europe is also losing ground to the United States, whose industry performs much better in the global market. This means that, to an ever increasing extent, the European leasing market is showing all the signs of a "mature market" and that expansion on the world markets is shifting towards the emerging economies. In the future development of the leasing market, we will therefore have to allow increasingly for the differences between developed and less developed economies.

In the modern industrialized countries, the economic structure is undergoing a steady shift towards a service economy, which in turn leads to a shift in the nature and scope of the demand for leasing. The decline in industrial activity in Western European countries will result in a decrease in demand for industrial capital goods. In contrast, however, there will be an increase in demand in the service sector for computer equipment, photocopiers, fax machines and telecommunications equipment. New applications for leasing will also emerge in expanding sectors such as health care.

In view of the lower capital requirements of the service sector, the shift from industry to services will probably have a negative effect on

---

[10] See World Leasing Year book 1995, page 4

leasing volume. In other words, the demand for leasing is likely to be greater in an industrial economy than in a service economy. This hypothesis has not as yet been supported by empirical research, but the figures do point in this direction. In this regard, it appears that the relative importance of the leasing of computer equipment in Europe is decreasing rather than increasing. In both 1993 and 1994, leasing volumes for computer equipment in Europe went down.[11] This decrease can partly be explained by the sharp drop in the price of computer equipment over the past few years. It is also striking that leasing volume in the service sector in Europe has shown a decline in both real and relative terms over the past few years. In 1994, for instance, the leasing market in Europe recovered in all sectors other than the service sector and government sector.

The considerably higher growth expectations for emerging economies present a very different picture from the mediocre prospects in Western Europe. Developments in these countries are important to the future leasing market for more than one reason. In the first place, these countries have the prospect of long-term and structurally high economic growth. The example of successfully developing economies in South-East Asia is rapidly being followed in South America.

While economic development in some of these countries is not yet always completely balanced, most countries are advocating a policy of restructuring government financing, curbing inflation and stimulating economic growth. In the light of a massive backlog in infrastructural development, huge investments in the field of civil engineering are in prospect. These will create a demand for the financing or leasing of the required construction machinery. In agriculture, too, these countries will play an increasingly important role in the global market. The combination of cheap land, cheap labor and modern technology will create great opportunities for these countries in the world market. The use of modern agricultural techniques will also entail the use of modern agricultural machinery, so these countries could of course become interesting in terms of leasing potential. Considering the size of countries like China, India, Brazil and Argentina, the volume of investment will be huge. The leasing potential is therefore considerable.

Against this background of huge market potential, we must also consider the relatively high risks in these countries. We are referring here not only to political and economic risks, but also to shortcomings in the legislation. Obviously, such risks must always be considered

11 See Leaseurope annual reports 1993 and 1994

carefully. An important aspect is therefore the extent to which leasing in these countries would provide solutions to reduce risk to an acceptable level. It is beyond doubt that an innovative leasing company should be able to think up appropriate solutions in this area. In some countries, for example in Eastern Europe, guarantee schemes for leasing are in place as part of the economic stimulation policy. It must therefore be concluded that these countries offer very attractive prospects for leasing.

6.3 CHANGES IN ECONOMIC STRUCTURE

In the future, changes in the economic structure of the various countries will also lead to developments in the leasing industry. Here, too, we should differentiate between industrialized countries and emerging economies. We have already mentioned the shift towards the service sector in industrialized countries and the effect this has on the nature and volume of demand for leasing. This is, however, just one aspect of the structural changes.

Another factor to consider is the shift in the typical size of companies. Business growth is no longer happening in the industrial giants, but more in the small and medium-sized enterprises (SMEs). This is partly due to the growth in the service sector, where SMEs are well represented, but is also due to the 'lean' policy of large companies and the trend towards decentralization in the form of creating independent business units. The process of outsourcing non-core activities should also be remembered here. All this is leading to a shift in activity in favor of the SMEs. In future, the leasing market will consequently shift its attention towards this group of companies.

The emergence of the smaller, more specialized companies will also lead to important changes in the area of logistics. The economic structure is increasingly developing in the direction of a network of specialized subcontractors. The customer base for these specialized companies is becoming ever more international. The emergence of specialized suppliers in a variety of locations obviously entails an increase in the transportation of both goods and people. Investment in every possible means of transport will increase rapidly in the coming years, and it is obvious that leasing will be able to benefit greatly from this.

At present, means of transport are already by far the most important category of leased assets. In Europe, cars now constitute approximately 40% of the leasing market, while trucks and trailers account for

14%. The figures from Leaseurope over the past few years show strong growth in the car sector; it is expected that similar growth will also be experienced in commercial vehicles.

6.4 TECHNOLOGICAL DEVELOPMENTS

Technological developments also have a major impact on the future of leasing, stemming from two key sources. On the one hand, technology influences the nature and quality of the objects subject to leasing. On the other hand, modern technology influences the way the leasing company will be run in future. The influence of modern information technology is the most important aspect here. We will deal with this in more detail in section 6.6; in the present section we will limit our discussion to the effect of technology on the nature and size of demand for leasing.

The impact on the demand side can most clearly be seen in the computer market. Because of the development of new generations of chips, the price of computer equipment has been falling considerably for some years. Ever better and cheaper equipment is arriving on the market, and the large mainframes of the past are gradually being replaced by cheaper PCs and networks. This development means lower volumes of investment and, consequently, a decrease in leasing volumes.

Furthermore, there has been a shift in the nature of investment from hardware to software. This shift will have a negative effect on the remarketing potential of computer equipment, and thus increases the residual value risks. Computer equipment is becoming obsolete at a more and more rapid pace, making it more difficult to manage the residual value risks for computer equipment. The overall impact is a steady decline leasing potential, particularly in the area of operating leases. The fall in the price of computer equipment, on the other hand, leads to an increase in demand, which partially compensates for the loss in revenue due to the decrease in investment volume.

The shift from hardware to software and the emergence of computer networks also influences the nature of investment. The emphasis is shifting from investment in equipment towards solving clients' information problems. The customer will demand an integrated solution for his information problems. This means that tailored solutions will have to be offered and that the supplier will increasingly find himself in a consultant's role. This development automatically means that the supplier is playing an increasingly important role in deciding whether or not a leasing solution will be chosen.

The emergence of digitalization will also have its effect on investment in other types of office equipment, such as photocopiers, printers and fax machines. Electronic data processing and the move towards the "paperless office" will increasingly result in systems replacing the function of photocopiers, faxes and printers. This, too, will mean a decrease in investment and leasing volume for this type of office equipment.

The development of modern information technology will therefore have far-reaching consequences for the office automation market, and with it the potential for leasing. It is difficult to estimate what the net effect on volume will be. After all, as we have mentioned, the decrease in investment volume as a result of falling prices also creates more demand. As a rule, increases occur in new markets which often require a totally different marketing approach.

An example of this is the mass market which has emerged in the field of computers and telecommunications. This market not only covers smaller companies, but also to a large extent that for private individuals. The question here is: what position will the leasing sector take up in these markets?

Aside from this, it will be interesting to see what kind of products the leasing sector will bring into play in future in response to the shift towards software investment. Will digitalization lead to expansion or contraction of the leasing sector? The answer will largely depend on the industry's innovative capabilities.

Another aspect of technological development is the increasing technical quality of machines, vehicles and equipment. Not only are improvements being constantly made in technical performance, the need for maintenance and repairs is fast declining. This development is particularly noticeable in the transport sector. Motor cars and trucks require fewer and fewer maintenance visits to garages.

As a result, the maintenance and repair of vehicles can be increasingly better planned and more suitable for financing as part of a (service) leasing contract. This development will therefore lead to a growth in the market for (full) service leasing. In addition, because of the increasing use of electronics in vehicles, maintenance and repair are becoming increasingly specialist jobs. For non-garages, in-house maintenance is becoming less and less attractive. For this reason, transport companies and in-house transporters will contract out fleet maintenance and management more and more in the future.

A further consequence of ever increasing technical quality is that loyalty to one specific brand is coming under pressure. As the quality offered by the various brands increases and / or differences in quality decrease, it is becoming easier for the customer to switch brands. When a competitor can no longer be warded off with quality, the next resort is often the price weapon. In these situations, leasing can be an attractive alternative, if only because the supplier is able to recoup part of the discount granted because of a favorable residual return value in the long run.

Another advantage of leasing is that a permanent relationship with the customer is maintained through the leasing contract. All these factors could result in leasing being used increasingly in the future as a marketing tool.

Developments in modern information technology also influence the pricing process in the leasing sector. After all, it is evident that modern information technology is leading to ever greater transparency in virtually all markets. As a result, it is becoming an increasingly simple matter to compare prices. Comparing prices via the Internet, for instance, will become easier and easier, and margins will come under increasing pressure. Moreover, market transparency in this context means that the composition of a product is also more transparent. The pricing of previously less transparent products such as "service products" will become clearer in the future. This will force suppliers to aim for maximum efficiency in their operations in order to stay competitive.

In this situation, the challenge is increasingly becoming to earn a premium with new products and services by offering added value beyond that offered by other producers in the market. In other words: modern information technology forces suppliers to seek market differentiation.

6.5 THE IMPACT OF LEGISLATION

The leasing market is highly sensitive to influences resulting from legislation. As indicated in Chapter 2, the following are the three key areas: fiscal legislation, civil legislation and accounting legislation.

The influence of fiscal legalization on leasing has always been very important. The tax authorities influence the cost price of leasing to a large extent, and therefore effect the attractiveness of the product. The criteria on which the fiscal authorities base their policies can be very diverse, mainly depending on government objectives in economic and budget policy.

Governments in favor of economic stimulation often apply tax-friendly measures, which can turn out favorably for leasing. Examples of these are the investment premiums that have been used in some European countries and in America. Leasing is often a good vehicle for obtaining the maximum benefit from such premium systems. Experience has taught us that leasing can grow significantly under the influence of a favorable fiscal regime.

In Western Europe, however, the days of expansive government policy are over and the approaching European Monetary Union is forcing most member states to adopt a very restrictive policy in order to comply with the conditions of the Maastricht Treaty. It is clear that, in Western Europe, tax-friendly measures for leasing can no longer be expected. In actual fact, the reverse is true: the budgetary problems of all the Western European governments invite measures which will have a negative effect. An example of this is the planned change by the Dutch Government in the legislation on "*bodemrecht*" (a landlord's right to distrain any goods and chattels found on his premises). This law regulates the priority which the tax authorities enjoy in the case of bankruptcy.

Until now, genuine title to a means of production in the case of operating leases offered reasonable protection against repossession by the tax authorities. This principle has now been contested by the tax authorities. Their argument is that leasing often infringes too much on the favored position of the tax office. It is obvious that this discussion of principle cannot be dissociated from the budgetary problems with which the government is faced. It is therefore to be expected that the tax authorities will take further measures if they feel that they are losing out because of leasing.

The same applies to cross-border leases. This refers to leasing contracts whereby a lessor in country A benefits from the fiscal situation in country B. The fiscal authorities are alert in assessing the economic reality of these transactions, and they will try and reverse this trend if it is felt that the transaction is motivated more by tax motives than by economic ones. Practice does indeed show that the playing-field for cross-border deals is becoming ever smaller.

Government policy in emerging economies obviously has different objectives. Leasing-friendly fiscal measures are more in evidence here, in view of the intended stimulation of the economy. Stimulation measures targeted at leasing not only provide a financial stimulus, but could also help solve the risk problems which often hamper investment in these countries. For emerging economies, leasing appears to be an effective way of stimulating investment which is still not being exploited as it should.

From a fiscal point of view, the conclusion is therefore that, in modern industrialized countries, government policy will be focusing on restrictive measures. This will not benefit the (fiscal) attractiveness of leasing. The effect of saturation in the European leasing market will thus be reinforced. In the emerging economies, we see the opposite happening. The potential for growth could be even further stimulated by a tax-friendly climate.

Civil legislation is very important for leasing in terms of regulating title. Liability aspects also play a role here. Leasing naturally benefits from a well-developed legal system, where title is well defined. In countries where this is not the case, the use of this instrument is seriously hampered. In this respect, the modern industrial countries have a distinct advantage over less developed economies. As a result, leasing in these countries often involves higher risks. These differences will diminish since all the emerging countries are advocating a market economy and, as a result, are being forced to adopt legislation in line with international standards.

Civil legislation also has an indirect effect on the leasing market, for example, in the case of legislation concerning the nature and quality of leased assets. A good example here is the transport sector. In the context of environmental policy, measures concerning the emission of exhaust fumes and noise pollution are increasingly being taken at European level. More stringent rules apply to the conditions under which foodstuffs may be transported. Such measures obviously have a negative effect on the residual value of vehicles which do not meet these new standards. This illustrates once again that bearing residual value risks is not in itself without risk.

These risks not only result from the difficulty in predicting the rate of technological obsolescence, but are also influenced by changes in legislation which are hard to predict and cannot be controlled.

This last aspect is particularly interesting, as it illustrates that the government itself (unintentionally) influences the residual value risk to a certain extent. It also sometimes forces leasing companies to run substantial residual value risks within the framework of fiscal directives on the difference between finance and operating leases.

The residual value issue also plays an important role in legislation in the field of accounting. Here, the key issue is where the line can be drawn with regard to economic risk. The rule is that the bearer of the economic risk of the object enters it as an asset on his balance sheet. In this case, economic risk is translated in terms of bearing the residual value risk. The practical application of this is expressed in rules on the maximum term of a contract (e.g., not more than 90% of its economic life) or the minimal residual value (for instance, at least 10% of the sum invested). Leasing contracts not conforming to these conditions will not be considered operating leases by accountants, which means that the assets concerned must be entered as assets on the lessee's balance sheet.

When applying these rules there is obviously an area of tension. In the world of the large international accountancy firms, it is extremely important to be able to work according to standard international rules. The result of this, however, is often in conflict with economic reality. There are major differences in the nature of residual value risks in the different lease object categories. For computer equipment, any residual value position almost certainly involves an economic risk. The remarketing value of such equipment can be reduced to zero within a relatively short space of time.

In the case of real estate leasing, another problem manifests itself. Long-running terms are usual here; normally ten to twenty years. Estimating residual values over such a long period is virtually impossible in this market. It has been shown that buildings are becoming economically obsolete at an ever faster pace. Residual value over such a long period therefore almost always represents a real economic risk. In other words: economic reality cannot easily be controlled.

The objective of the international accountancy world to set standard international rules on economic risk could, in actual fact, prove a hindrance to the leasing world. The principal question here is whether expressing hard-to-assess risks in a couple of simple rules can possibly reflect economic reality. In a world of ever increasing specialization and increasingly rapid economic and technical obsolescence, this idea is unlikely to be fully tenable. We must expect the tension between accountants and leasing companies to increase in the future.

6.6 POTENTIAL CUSTOMERS' WILLINGNESS TO LEASE

The future of leasing is obviously also determined to a great extent by the willingness of (potential) customers to take leases. The issue here concerns the attractiveness of the lease product to the customer, and the future developments that can be expected in this regard.

In the preceding pages we have dealt with many aspects of great importance to the customer's willingness to lease. There are a number of other factors influencing the attractiveness of leasing for the customer, both now and in the future. These are mainly concerned with the nature and intensity of the processes of change in the economy, and their effects on the leasing market.

In every industry, the customer is observed to be continually setting higher demands on the quality of goods and services. This means that suppliers of products are constantly having to improve. Often, this is expressed in an improved price/quality ratio. In other words: the customer is getting better and better value for money. This trend is also noticeable in leasing.

A second aspect is that the diversity of supply is growing all the time. Some years back, a grocer could, for instance, make do with a product mix of approximately 800 articles. A supermarket today can easily have an assortment of around 15,000 articles. This increased diversity can be observed in all markets. It also involves ever increasing individualization of products.

Goods and services are becoming more and more "tailored". In some instances this is taken to extremes, where goods are produced exclusively on the basis of individual customer specifications. The American car manufacturer Saturn already uses this system, which is known as mass production with lot size 1.

A third aspect is that changes in the economy are taking place ever faster. This makes it more difficult than ever to predict market demand. Because of this, flexibility is an increasingly important feature of modern business strategy. The ability to adapt quickly to changing market conditions is becoming an ever more important success factor in business policy, so any factors limiting flexibility entail risk.

It goes without saying that the increasing need for flexibility represents an opportunity for leasing. In the future, the customer will be demanding more and more (temporary) solutions for the availability of machines, vehicles and equipment. Leasing is faced with the challenge of offering good solutions to meet this need. This also implies taking over risks from the customer, in particular those of residual value. It also makes it necessary to extend service provision and push the boundaries of leasing forward.

Another aspect of the market developments described above is that each manufacturer will focus more and more on his core business. It would not be exaggerating too much to suggest that the successful company of the future will have to be the best as well as the cheapest in its particular field. This means that each manufacturer will have to do its utmost to lower costs and raise quality. In the context of willingness to lease, this means that leasing will have to be cheaper and better than any other available alternative. The future of leasing will partly depend on whether it succeeds in meeting this requirement.

This requirement is possibly easier to meet in less-developed economies than in the modern industrialized countries. In the emerging economies, the supply structure is by definition under-developed, and it is easier to find a suitable leasing solution. In the developed economies we have a wide range of products, in some cases saturated markets, margins under pressure and customers demanding a better product for the same price. It is obvious that this area represents a great challenge for the future.

6.7 THE MARKETING POLICY OF LEASING COMPANIES

We will conclude this chapter by considering the marketing policy of leasing companies. It goes without saying that this policy determines the future of leasing to a large extent. In Chapter 3, we described marketing issues as the way in which a company meets certain market demands. We characterized the objective of marketing as creating the optimum link between the supply of goods and services on the one hand and the wishes of the customer on the other.

The question now is: how far will leasing be able to accomplish this task in the future? At this point, we should reflect for a moment on the position leasing holds in the market today. Leasing today is still predominantly offered in the form of finance leases. The McKinsey study indicated that, three years ago, 89% of the leasing portfolio in Europe consisted of finance leases. In the next three years it is expected that the share of finance leases in the portfolio will drop to 81%. From these figures, it appears that the shift towards more operating leases is still very tentative.

The predominance of finance leases can be seen as an indication that leasing has not as yet reached maturity. Leasing is, in many cases, still strongly associated with finance companies and is often seen as a special form of financing. This obviously does not do justice to the added value of leasing, and in a sense is holding back its development.

Developments in the market are, however, forcing leasing to change. The leasing sector can no longer be satisfied with offering products which do not stand out sufficiently from comparable products offered by banks. The customer has new and above all more demanding needs, and the future of leasing will depend on how far these new needs can be met.

In order to earn a good position in the market of the future, leasing companies will have to start putting marketing high on their list of priorities. This has clearly been lacking in the past: marketing has been undervalued for too long in the leasing sector. The McKinsey study of the European leasing sector has demonstrated this quite clearly once again.

Focusing on marketing starts by focusing on the customer. Getting a good picture of developments in market demand is the next step; not just a momentary snapshot, but also a vision of the future.

The process of change affecting leasing is very comprehensive. Markets are becoming more dynamic, but also more complex. With such a multitude of factors, it is impossible to excel in all fields. Choices will have to be made. These choices start with establishing which core competences a company possesses. In other words: where do we provide excellent performance?

Strategic objectives should then be formulated. What ambitions does the company have in the market, what are the company's goals, in what time-frame and in what way? With any strategic choice, it will be evident that two elements always play an important role: controlling or reducing costs and increasing the added value of the product. The need to consider both elements at all times stems from the fact that the market demands both cost and quality benefits.

Box 6.2

SUMMARY OF MARKET DEVELOPMENTS

In the preceding pages, we have mentioned a large number of relevant market developments. In summary, the following aspects are the most important:

- Changes in the market are taking place at an ever increasing pace;
- Changes in the market are becoming increasingly difficult to forecast;
- Customer wishes are becoming more and more diverse;
- The trend towards outsourcing non-core activities is on the increase;
- The need for flexibility is growing in all markets;
- The customer is increasingly demanding tailored solutions;
- The customer's quality requirements are continuously increasing;
- The customer wants a better product at the lowest possible price;
- Markets are becoming more and more transparent;
- Modern information technology is going to play an ever larger role;
- Markets in Western Europe are showing signs of saturation;
- Growth in the world market is shifting towards the emerging economies;
- Business is increasingly shifting towards small and medium-sized companies;
- The software component in many lease objects is getting larger;
- Legislation is becoming ever stricter.

For the leasing sector, cost benefits mean, amongst other things, being able to offer cheap funding and having an efficient organization. The added value of the product can be improved in various ways, of which just a few examples are listed here:

- expanding service components;
- expanding services to include consultancy;
- faster acceptance;
- more effective utilization of distribution channels;

- more international services;
- introduction of new leasing applications;
- improving information provision.

Increasing added value and lowering costs obviously do not always go together. However, the two objectives can be combined to some extent, certainly through the application of modern information technology. As an example of development in this field, look at the banking and insurance sector. A real revolution is taking place here as a result of the application of modern electronics. Its influence is expanding rapidly, from automation of the back-office to automation of the front-office. A phenomenon like electronic banking leads to an increasing number of products and services being sold through electronic media.

The benefits are many and will result in considerable cost savings, a better level of service (24 hour banking facilities), faster and better provision of information to the customer, and a huge expansion in the nature of the services offered. There is no doubt that such a development will also take place in leasing. The use of modern electronics in leasing offers the following possibilities:

- Lowering operating costs;
- Increasing processing capacity for (large) payment flows;
- Expansion of the scope of leasing to include smaller transactions (small ticket leasing);
- Better and faster provision of information;
- Expansion of the product range with new (full) service and information products;
- Faster and better debtor assessment (credit check);
- More flexible contract conditions;
- Use of new distribution channels.

Given the development costs of modern systems, there is likely to be a strong tendency towards concentration in the leasing sector. Particularly good prospects can be expected for bank-allied leasing companies, which should, after all, benefit from the synergy effects in the use of electronics in the banking business and in leasing.

Modern electronics also offers possibilities for suppliers to use leasing more efficiently through their own distribution channels. Independent suppliers will find it increasingly difficult to survive in the marketplace of the future. The influence of modern information technology will culminate in a situation where there is only scope for suppliers with large capital resources, good systems, and distinctive advantages in the field of distribution.

Another aspect of the trade-off between cost control and quality improvement is the choice between doing it in-house or outsourcing. Leasing companies, like their customers, will have to think about what their core business is and which activities could better be outsourced. This question is becoming ever more important as the market demands ever higher standards of service. Expanding service provision is only the right way to go if the supplier is able to offer these services at competitive rates. Every area of the market, however, is shifting towards further specialization, and that includes the services offered by leasing companies. In many cases, expansion of service provision will have to be effected through joint-ventures. Partnerships with suppliers (and with customers) will thus become increasingly important in the future, which is why we have given such detailed consideration to this aspect.

In a dynamic environment, the ability to adapt quickly to changing market conditions is a crucial factor for success. Apart from investing in know-how and good systems, which any lease company should be doing, this aspect is of primary importance. To make this happen, the question of how best to promote innovation and creativity in the organization needs to be considered. Good ideas do not just appear out of the blue.

Innovation and creativity can be applied in an organization as a matter of policy and strategy. This is also an important area of attention for the management of leasing companies who wish to place marketing high on their priority list.

The theme of leasing and marketing is a fascinating and challenging subject. Interesting yet difficult challenges await managers who really want to get to grips with this subject. It is difficult to predict the future, but, in the long term, ignoring the fact that the rules of the game have changed can only result in being knocked out of the competition. If you want to stay in the match, you must have the courage to take chances - or risk being eliminated yourself.

There is no middle course.

References

Ansoff, H.I., *"Corporate Strategy"*, McGraw-Hill Books International, 1995.

Baker, D.D., *"Lease versus Buy: Avoid Excess Costs"*, Management Accounting, 77(1), 1995.

Beckman, H. and A.W.A., *"Leasing van roerend en onroerend goed"*, Stenfert Kroese, Leiden / Antwerpen, 1980.

Beckman, H. (ed.), *"Handboek leasing"*, Kluwer Bedrijfswetenschappen, loose-leaf manual.

Branson, B.C., *"An Empirical Reexamination of the Leasing Puzzle"*, Quarterly Journal of Business and Economics, 34(3), 1995.

Buckland, M., A. Woodworth and J.F. Williams, *"Managing the Economics of Owing, Leasing and Contracting out Information Services"*, Information Processing and Management, 31(1), 1995.

Business Week, *Articles.*

Cazals, P., *"New Forms of Financing; Leasing and Concessions"*, Rail International, 26(8-9), 1995.

Drury, C., *"Lease Financing"*, MCB, Bradford, 1989.

Durinck, E., *"Financial leasing: concept, accounting and tax aspects"*, UFI, Antwerpen, 1991.

Durinck, E., *"Financial Leasing and the pie approach"*, UFI, Antwerpen, 1991.

Ely, K.M.M., *"Operating Lease Accounting and the Market's Assessment of Equity Risk"*, Journal of Accounting Research, 33(2), 1995.

Fortune, *Articles.*

Gabele, E. and M. Kroll, *"Leasingvertraege Optimal Gestalten"*, Gabler, Wiesbaden, 1992.

Gao, S.S., *"International leasing: its financial and accounting application"*, UCL Publications, Preston, 1994

Grant, R. and D. Gent, *"Asset Finance and Leasing Handbook"*, Woodhead-Faulkner, New York, 1992.

Grenadier, S.R., *"Valuing Lease Contracts: A real-options Approach"*, Journal of Financial Economies, 38(3), 1995.

Hagger, E., *"Leasing - The Pickle Lease had Become the Market's Darling, with ever Increasing Volumes and Deal Types"*, Corporate Finance, (130), 1995.

Hamel, G. and C.K. Prahalad, *"Competing for the Future"*, Harvard Business School Press, 1994.

Jagersma, P.K., *"Internationaal Management"*, Stenfert Kroese, Houten, 1996.

Kotler, Ph. and A. Andreasen, *"Strategic Marketing for Non-Profit Organizations"*, Prentice-Hall, Englewood Cliffs, New York, 1991.

Kotler, Ph., *"Marketing Management"*, 8th edition, Prentice-Hall, Englewood Cliffs, New York, 1994.

Kramer, A., *"Neue Vertragsformen der Wirtschaft; Leasing, Factoring, Franchising"*, Bern, 1985.

Leaseurope and Arthur Andersen, *"Leasing in Europe"*, McGraw-Hill Book Company Europe, 1992.

Leaseurope and Coopers&Lybrand, *"A Practical Guide to Leasing"*, McGraw-Hill Book Company Europe, 1994.

Leaseurope, Annual reports.

Lee, K., *"Optimal Lease contracts"*, Regional Science and Urban Economics, 25(6), 1995.

Miller, S.E., *"The Economics of Automobile Leasing"*, The Journal of Consumer Affairs, 29(1), 1995.

Morrison, R., *"Loan or Lease? A question of Needs"*, Pit and Quarry, 88(6), 1995.

Palmer, A., *"Principles of Services Marketing"*, McGraw-Hill Books International, 1994.

Porter, M.E., *"Competitive Advantage"*, The Free Press, New York, 1985.

Porter, M.E., "*The Competitive Advantage of Nations*", The MacMillan Press Ltd., London, 1992.

Schallheim, J.S., "*Lease or buy?; Principles for Sound Decision-making*", Harvard Business School Press, Mass., 1994.

Schallheim, J.S. and L.D. Schall, "*Lease or Buy*", The Journal of Finance, 50(5), 1995.

Sharpe, S.S. and H.N. Nguyen, "*Capital Market Imperfections and the Incentive to Lease*", Journal of Financial Economics, 39(2-3), 1995.

Sliter, T., "*Lease for Less*", The Local Area Network Magazine, 10(4), 1995.

Soper, D.R. and R.M. Munro, "*The Leasing Handbook*", McGraw-Hill, New York, 1991.

Tirard, J., " *Tax-leveraged leasing*", Bulletin for International Fiscal Documentation, 49, 1995.

Vries, de W., Kasper, H. and P. van Helsdingen, "*Dienstenmarketing*", Educatieve Partners Nederland / Stenfert Kroese, Houten, 1994.

Wainman, "*Leasing*", Waterlow Publishers, London, 1991.

Williamson, S.D., "*A New Lease*", Progressive Railroading, 38(11), 1995.

Wolfert, F., "*Practical Leasing Strategies to Improve Financial Efficiency*", TMA Journal, 15(6), 1995.

Woodsworth, A. and J.F. Williams, "*Managing the Economics of Owing, Leasing and Contracting out Information Services*", Aldershot, Ashgate, 1993.

World Leasing Yearbook 1995, Euromoney Publications plc., 1995.

About the book and the authors

Over the last few years, leasing industry managers have increasingly come to the realization that marketing must form an integral part of their companies' strategies. Markets today change very rapidly and clients are more and more demanding, all of which presents managers with the difficult challenge of prospering in this new environment. Clearly, the time when leasing companies could float along relying exclusively on experience and intuition has passed.

On the basis of survey material, this book offers an examination of the industry and possible company response strategies. Its authors see the need for active and long-term management of companies' partnerships with their clients and provide approaches to this end.

But this book is not only aimed at giving leasing companies the impetus to fully incorporate marketing into their strategies to help them face the future. As a study of the strategic marriage of leasing and marketing, it is also directed at other groups - such as consultants and academics - with an interest in this field.

Pieter Klaas Jagersma works in the Amsterdam office of McKinsey & Company, while Toon Sanders is a director in the Eindhoven office of De Lage Landen.

www.ingramcontent.com/pod-product-compliance
Lightning Source LLC
Chambersburg PA
CBHW051151180926
51611CB00001B/24
* 9 7 8 9 0 3 6 1 9 8 0 6 6 *